PAUL McCARTNEY

all the best!

ART DIRECTION AND DESIGN:
MICHAEL ROSS / Normal Service

Cover Photography:
Tim O'Sullivan

Illustrations:
Ian Beck, Jeff Dunbar, Bush Hollyhead, Paul Leith,
Ainslie Macleod, Michael Ross, Willie Ryan, David de Silva, Ian Wright

ISBN 978-1-4234-6320-7

A PUBLICATION OF

MPL COMMUNICATIONS, INC.
http://www.mplcommunications.com

EXCLUSIVELY DISTRIBUTED BY

HAL•LEONARD®
CORPORATION
7777 W. BLUEMOUND RD. P.O. BOX 13819 MILWAUKEE, WI 53213

For all works contained herein:
Unauthorized copying, arranging, adapting, recording, Internet posting, public performance,
or other distribution of the printed music in this publication is an infringement of copyright.
Infringers are liable under the law.

Visit Hal Leonard Online at
www.halleonard.com

STRUM AND PICK PATTERNS

This chart contains the suggested strum and pick patterns that are referred to by number at the beginning of each song in this book. The symbols ⊓ and ∨ in the strum patterns refer to down and up strokes, respectively. The letters in the pick patterns indicate which right-hand fingers plays which strings.

p = thumb
i = index finger
m = middle finger
a = ring finger

For example; Pick Pattern 2
is played: thumb - index - middle - ring

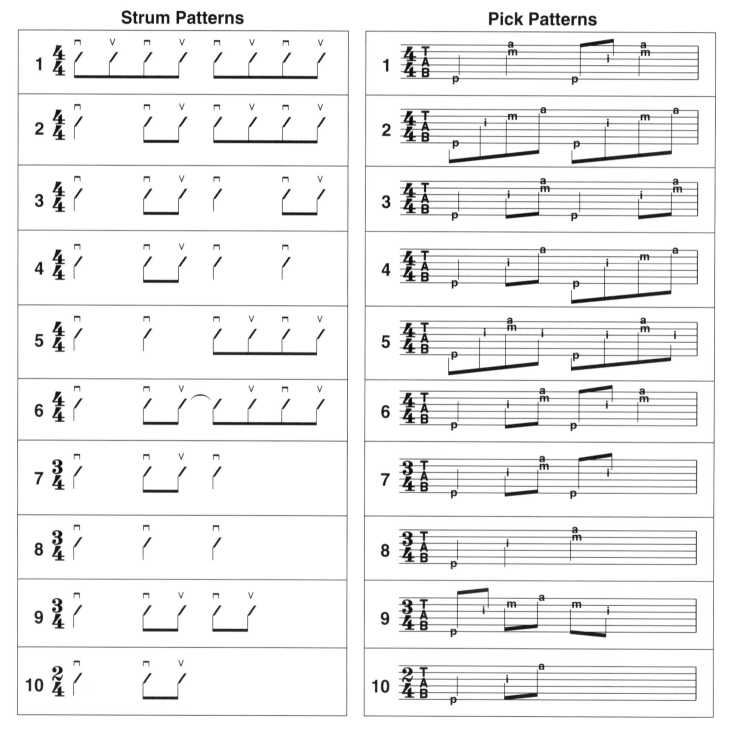

You can use the 3/4 Strum or Pick Patterns in songs written in compound meter (6/8, 9/8, 12/8, etc.).
For example, you can accompany a song in 6/8 by playing the 3/4 pattern twice in each measure.
The 4/4 Strum and Pick Patterns can be used for songs written in cut time (¢) by doubling the note time values in the patterns. Each pattern would therefore last two measures in cut time.

Band on the Run

Words and Music by Paul and Linda McCartney

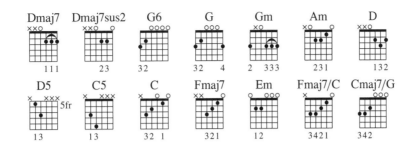

Strum Pattern: 1, 2
Pick Pattern: 6

Intro
Slowly

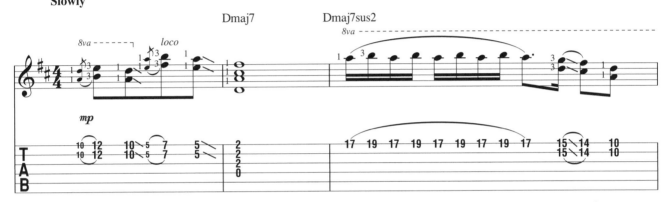

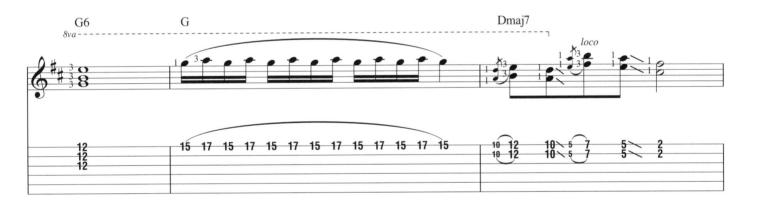

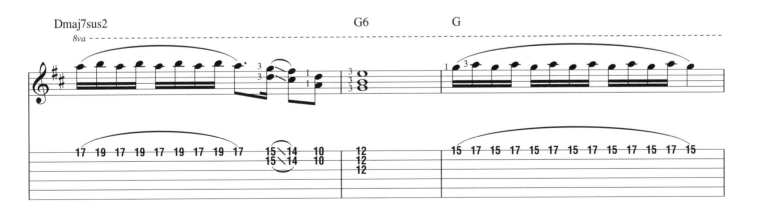

© 1974 (Renewed) PAUL and LINDA McCARTNEY
Administered by MPL COMMUNICATIONS, INC.
All Rights Reserved

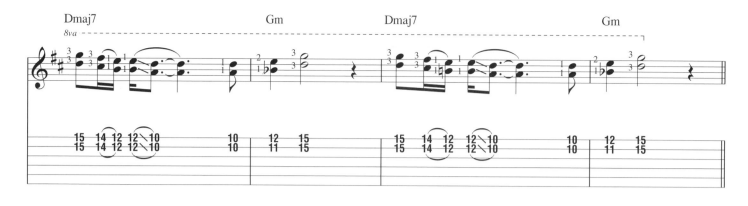

Verse

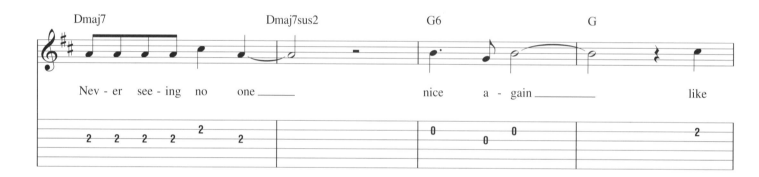

1. Stuck in - side these four walls. ____ Sent in - side for - ev - er. ____

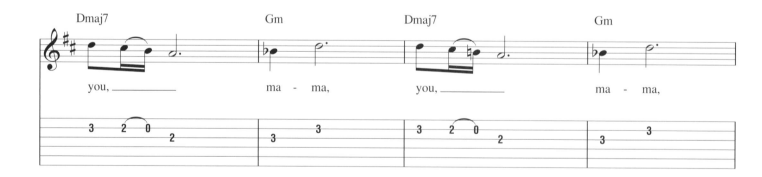

Nev - er see - ing no one _____ nice a - gain _____ like

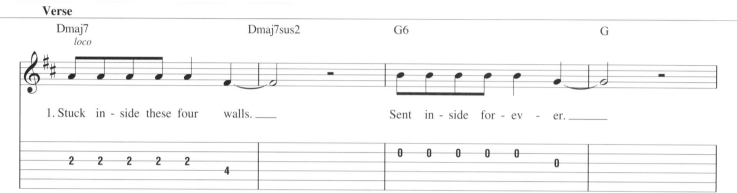

you, _____ ma - ma, you, _____ ma - ma,

Interlude

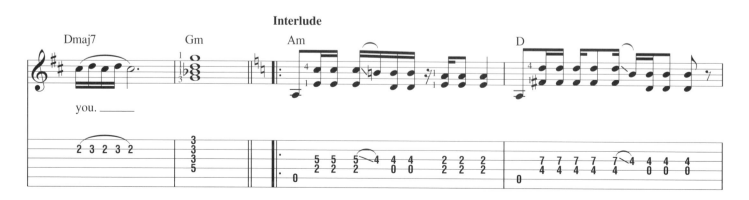

you. ____

Verse

2. If I ev - er get out ___ of here, thought of giv - ing at all ___ a - way ___

to a reg - is - tered char - i - ty. ___ All I need is a pint ___ a day. ___ If I

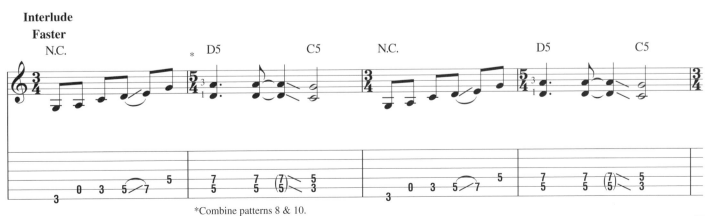

ev - er get out ___ of here. ___ (If we ev - er get out ___ of here.)

Interlude
Faster

*Combine patterns 8 & 10.

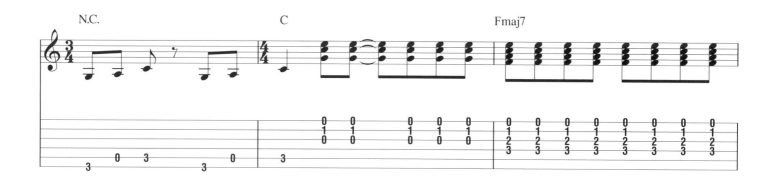

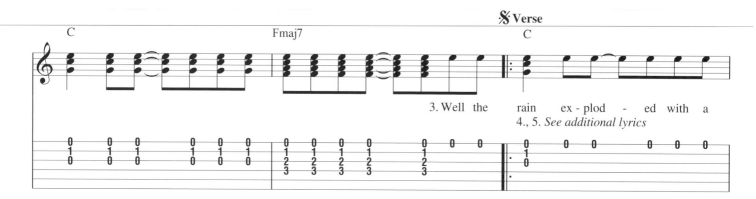

Verse

3. Well the rain ex-plod-ed with a

4., 5. *See additional lyrics*

might-y crash __ as we fell in-to __ the sun. And the

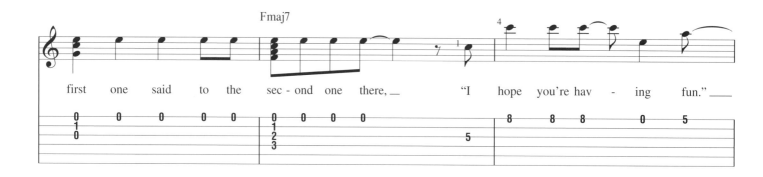

first one said to the sec-ond one there, __ "I hope you're hav-ing fun." __

Chorus

Band on the run, __

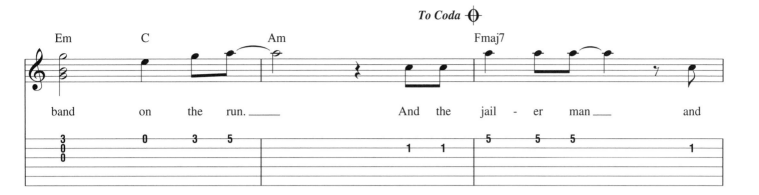

band　　　　on　　　the　　run.＿＿＿＿＿＿　　　　And　the　jail - er　man＿＿　　　and

Sail - or　Sam＿＿　　were　search - ing　ev - 'ry - one＿＿＿＿＿＿＿　　for　the

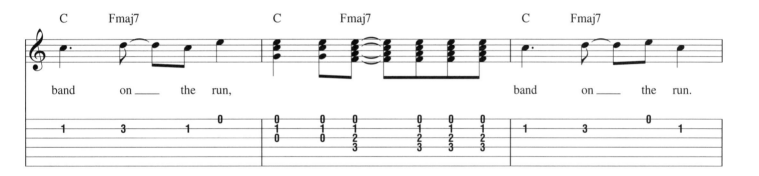

band　　　on＿＿　the　run,　　　　　　　　　　　band　　　on＿＿　the　run.

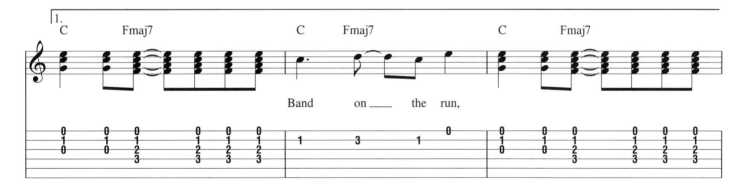

Band　　　on＿＿　the　run,

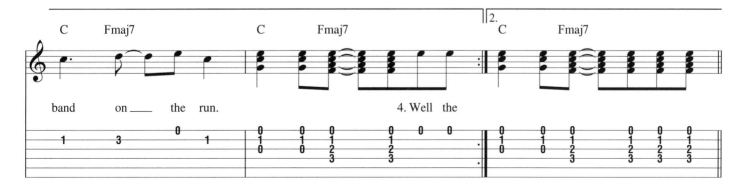

band　　　on＿＿　the　run.　　　　　　　　4. Well　the

Interlude

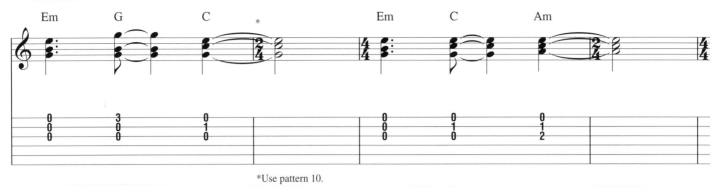

*Use pattern 10.

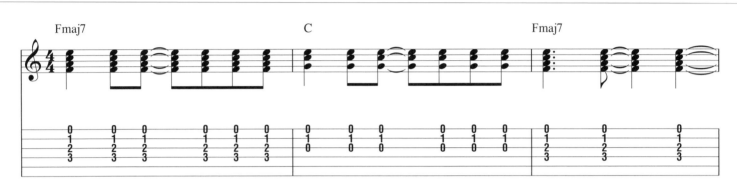

Chorus

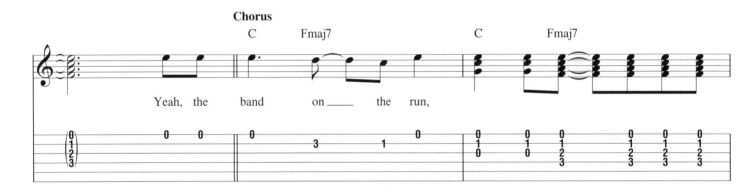

Yeah, the band on ___ the run,

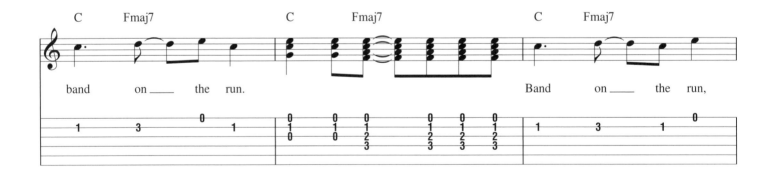

band on ___ the run.   Band on ___ the run,

D.S. al Coda

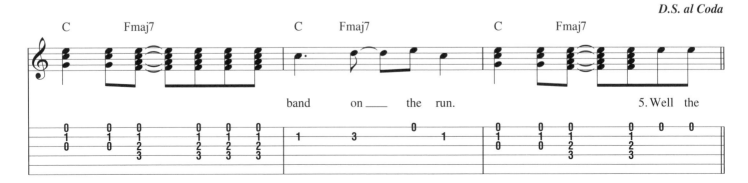

band on ___ the run.   5. Well the

⊕ Coda

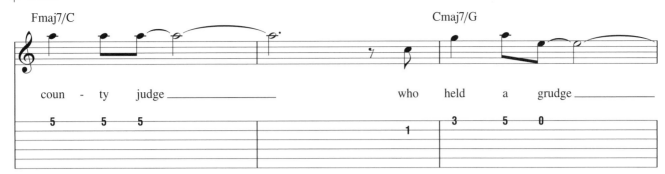

coun - ty judge _____ who held a grudge _____

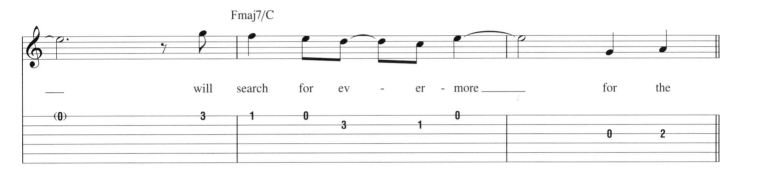

___ will search for ev - er - more _____ for the

Chorus

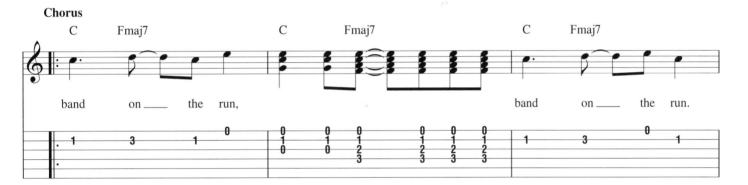

band on ___ the run, band on ___ the run.

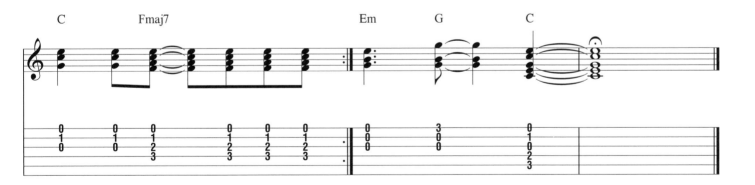

Additional Lyrics

4. Well, the undertaker drew a heavy sigh
   Seeing no one else had to come.
   And a bell was ringing in the village square
   For the rabbits on the run.

5. Well, the night was falling as the desert world
   Began to settle down.
   In the town they're searching for us ev'rywhere,
   But we never will be found.

Jet

Words and Music by Paul and Linda McCartney

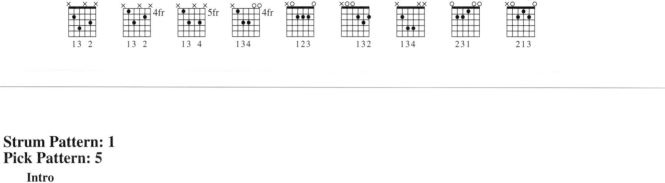

Strum Pattern: 1
Pick Pattern: 5

Intro
Moderately

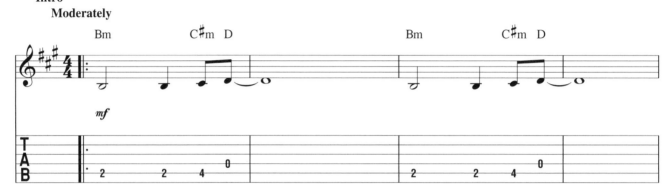

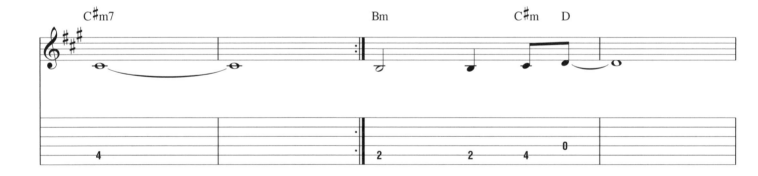

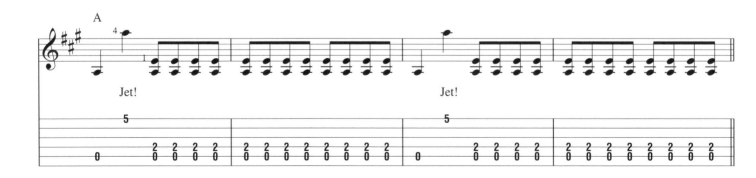

© 1974 (Renewed) PAUL and LINDA McCARTNEY
Administered by MPL COMMUNICATIONS, INC.
All Rights Reserved

Verse

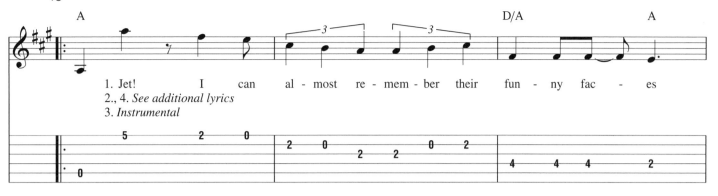

1. Jet! I can al - most re - mem - ber their fun - ny fac - es
2., 4. *See additional lyrics*
3. *Instrumental*

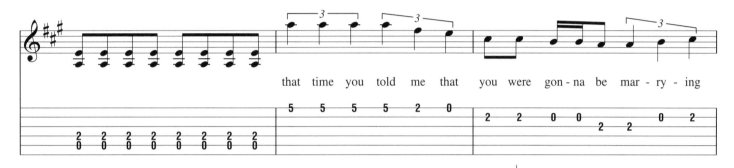

that time you told me that you were gon - na be mar - ry - ing

To Coda 2

Chorus

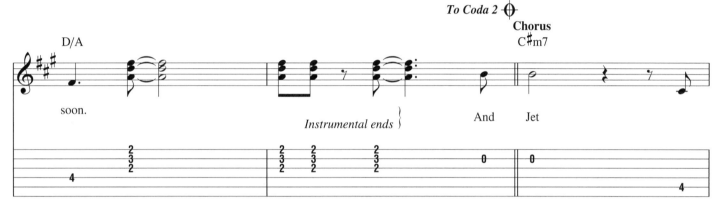

soon.

Instrumental ends And Jet

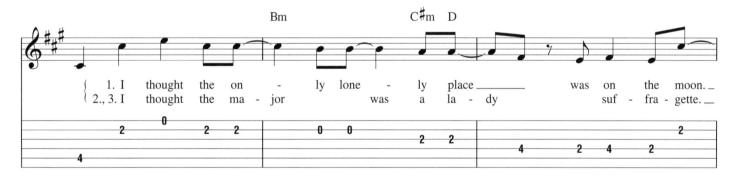

{ 1. I thought the on - ly lone - ly place _____ was on the moon. _____
{ 2., 3. I thought the ma - jor was a la - dy suf - fra - gette. _____

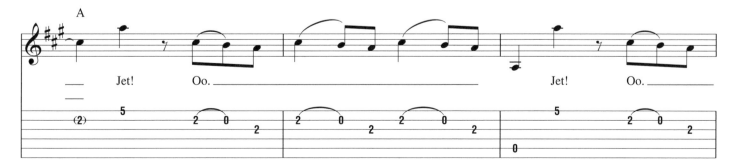

_____ Jet! Oo. _____ Jet! Oo. _____

Bridge

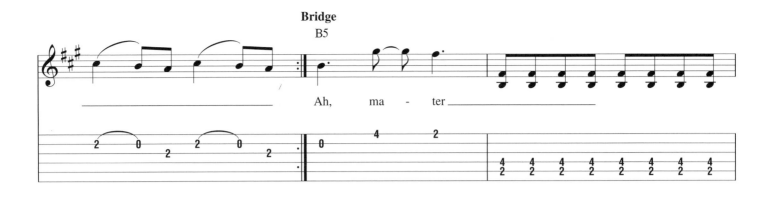

Ah, ma - ter _____

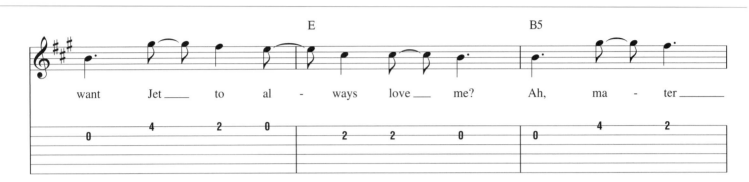

want Jet ___ to al - ways love ___ me? Ah, ma - ter _____

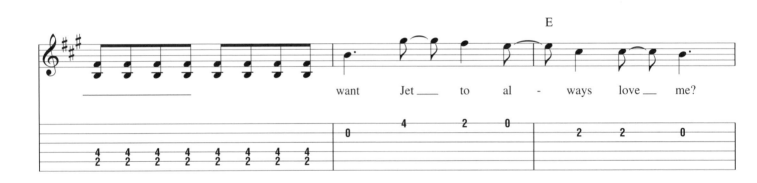

want Jet ___ to al - ways love ___ me?

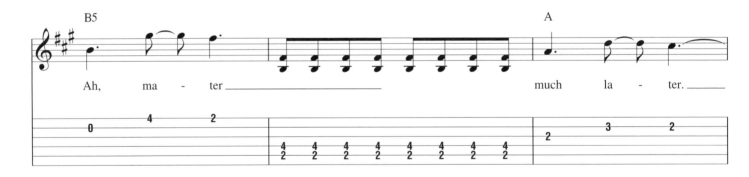

Ah, ma - ter _____ much la - ter. _____

Interlude

To Coda 1 ⊕

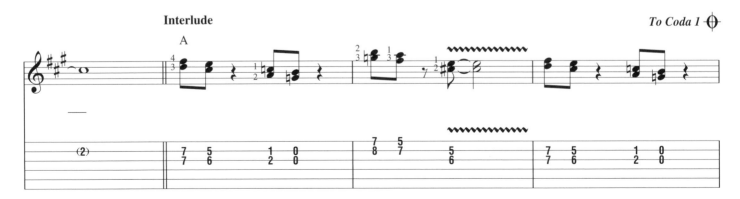

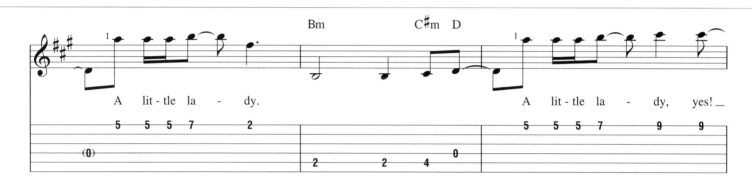

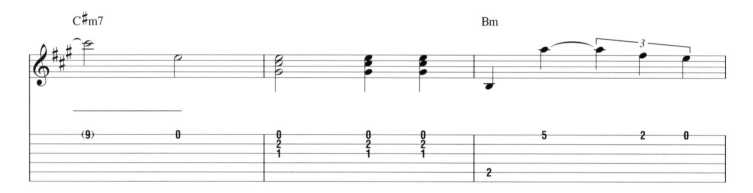

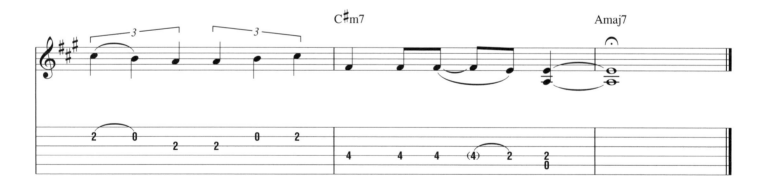

Additional Lyrics

2. Jet! Was your father as bold as a sergeant major?
   How come he told you that you were hardly old enough yet?

4. Jet! With the wind in your hair of a thousand laces.
   Climb on the back, and we'll go for a ride in the sky.

Listen to What the Man Said

Words and Music by Paul and Linda McCartney

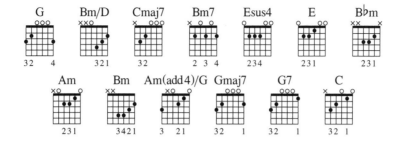

Strum Pattern: 4
Pick Pattern: 3

Intro
Moderately fast

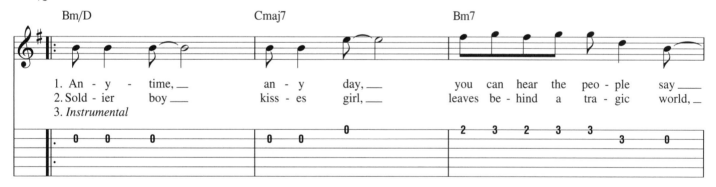

1. An - y - time, __ an - y day, __ you can hear the peo - ple say __
2. Sold - ier boy __ kiss - es girl, __ leaves be - hind a tra - gic world, __
3. *Instrumental*

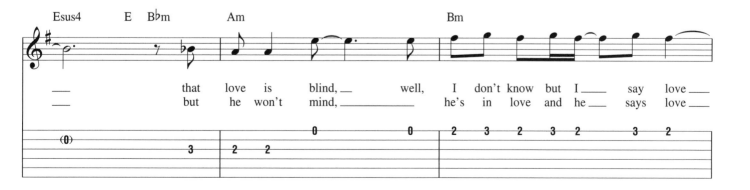

that love is blind, __ well, I don't know but I __ say love __
but he won't mind, _____ he's in love and he __ says love __

© 1975 (Renewed) MPL COMMUNICATIONS, INC.
All Rights Reserved

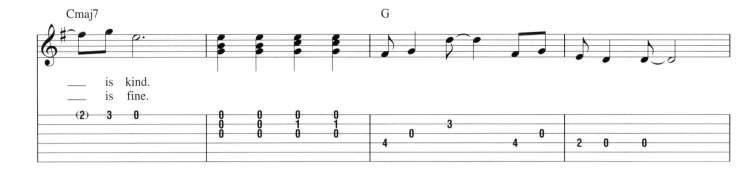

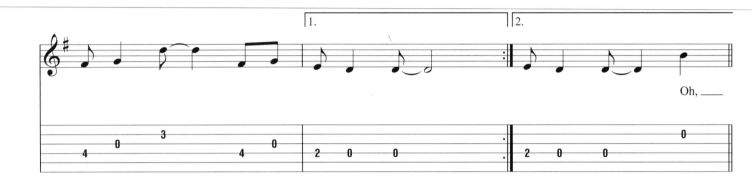

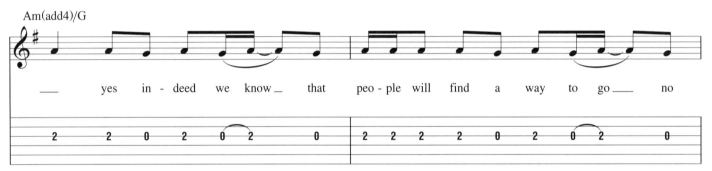

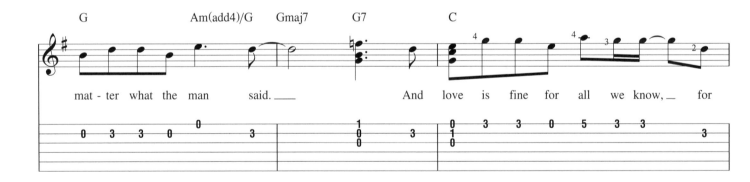

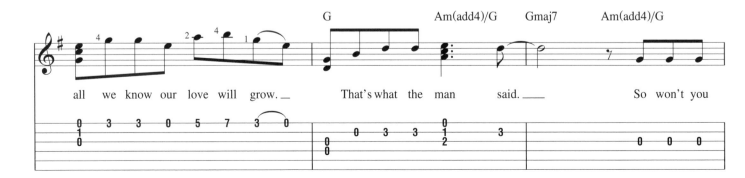

Ebony and Ivory

Words and Music by Paul McCartney

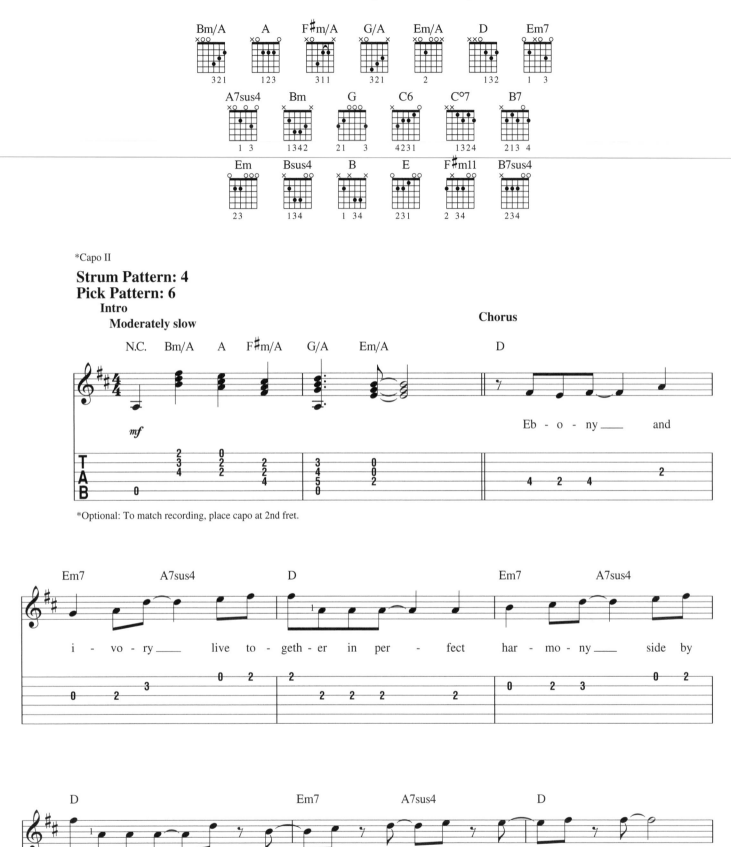

*Capo II

Strum Pattern: 4
Pick Pattern: 6

Intro

Moderately slow

Chorus

*Optional: To match recording, place capo at 2nd fret.

© 1982 MPL COMMUNICATIONS, INC.
All Rights Reserved

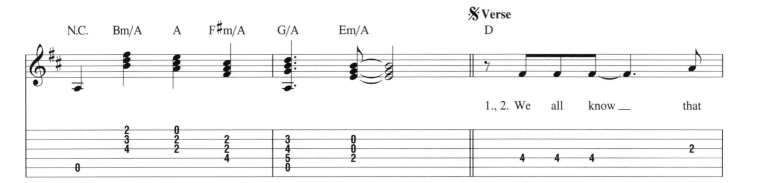

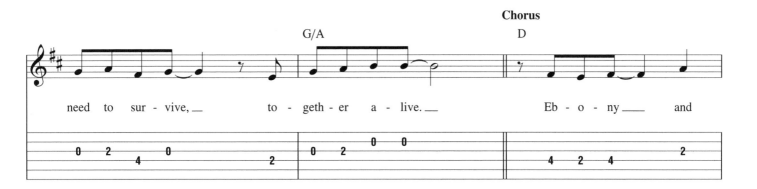

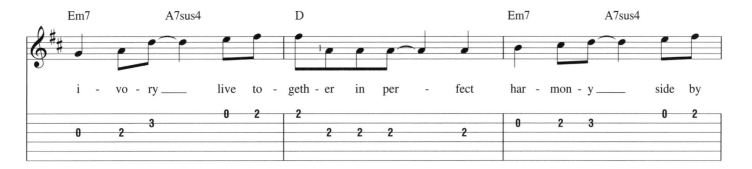

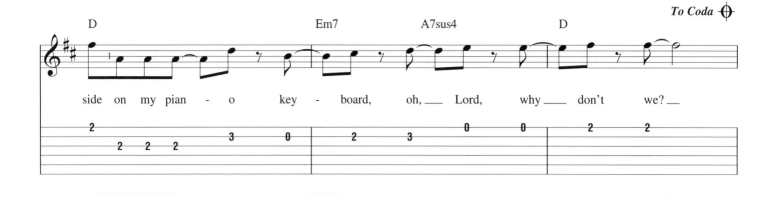

side on my pian - o key - board, oh, ___ Lord, why ___ don't we? ___

Interlude

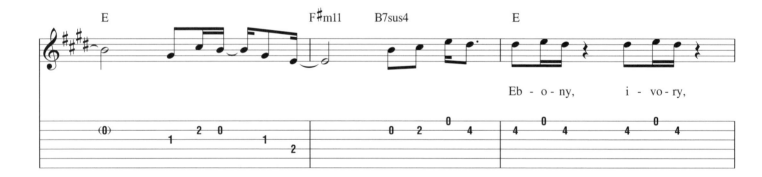

Eb - o - ny, i - vo - ry,

D.S. al Coda

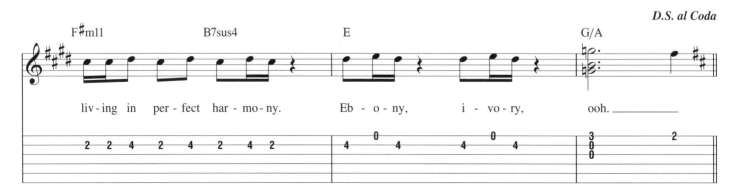

liv - ing in per - fect har - mo - ny. Eb - o - ny, i - vo - ry, ooh. _____

Coda

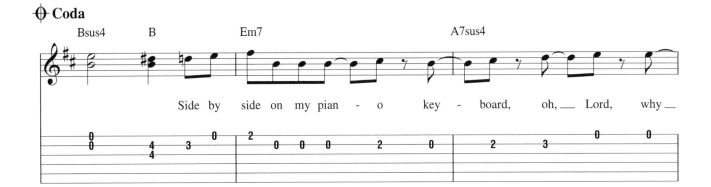

Side by side on my pian - o key - board, oh, __ Lord, why __

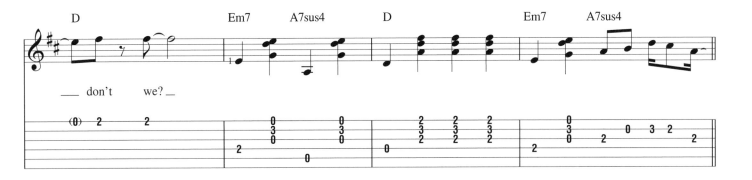

__ don't we? __

Interlude

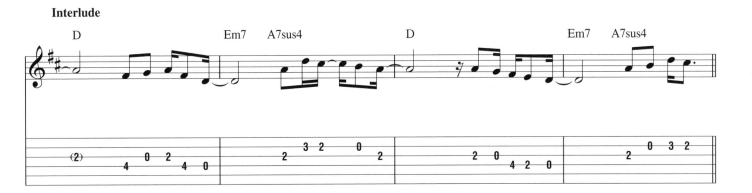

Outro

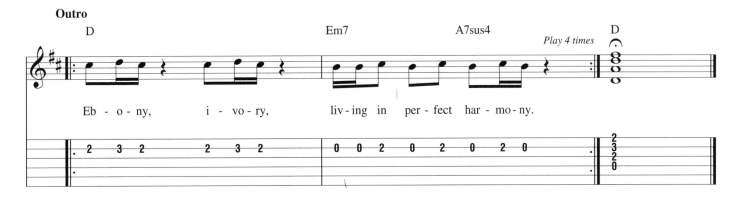

Eb - o - ny, i - vo - ry, liv - ing in per - fect har - mo - ny.

No More Lonely Nights

from the Motion Picture GIVE MY REGARDS TO BROAD STREET

Words and Music by Paul McCartney

*Tune down 1 step:
(low to high) D-G-C-F-A-D

Strum Pattern: 4
Pick Pattern: 4

Verse

Moderately

*Optional: To match recording, tune down 1 step.

1. I can wait an-oth-er day ___ un - til I call ___ you,

you've on - ly got my heart on a string ___ and ev -'ry-thing ___ a - flut - ter.

*Use Pattern 10.

𝄋 Verse

2. But an - oth - er lone - ly night ___ might take for - ev -

3. *See additional lyrics*
4. *Instrumental*

© 1984 MPL COMMUNICATIONS, INC.
All Rights Reserved

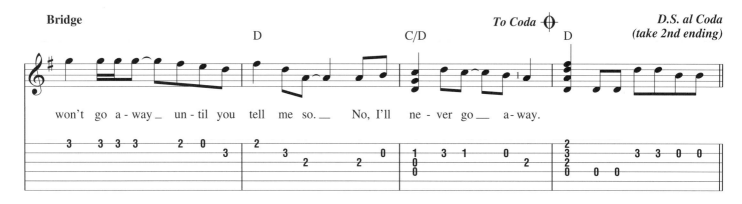

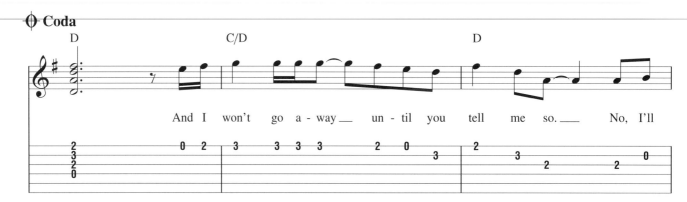

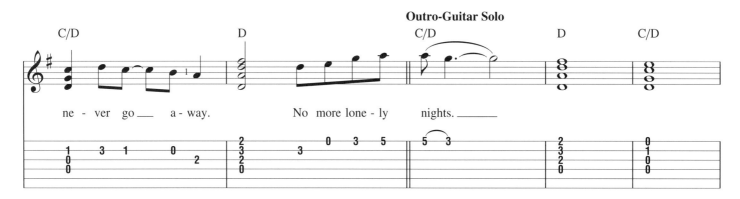

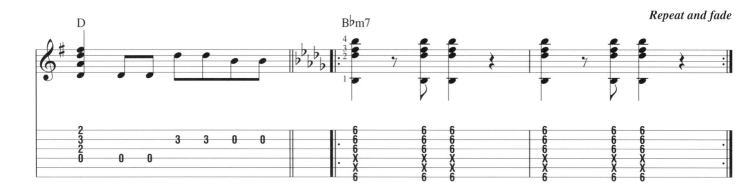

Additional Lyrics

3. May I never miss the thrill
Of being near you.
And if it takes a couple of years
To turn your tears to laughter…

Another Day

Words and Music by Paul and Linda McCartney

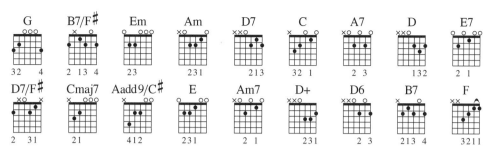

Strum Pattern: 1, 6
Pick Pattern: 4, 5

Verse

Moderately

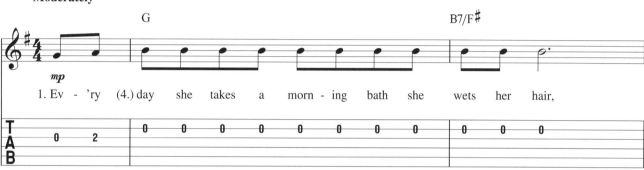

1. Ev - 'ry (4.) day she takes a morn - ing bath she wets her hair,

wraps a tow'l a - round her as she's head - ing for the bed - room chair. It's just an - oth - er day.

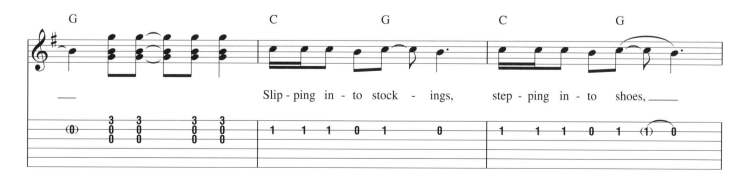

Slip - ping in - to stock - ings, step - ping in - to shoes,

© 1971 (Renewed) PAUL and LINDA McCARTNEY
Administered by MPL COMMUNICATIONS, INC.
All Rights Reserved

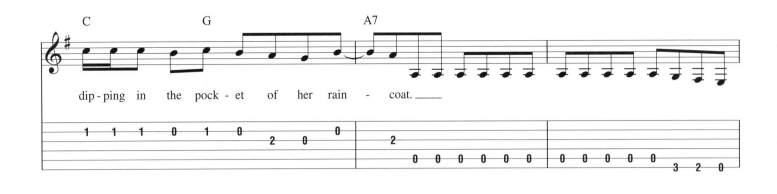

dip - ping in the pock - et of her rain - coat. ____

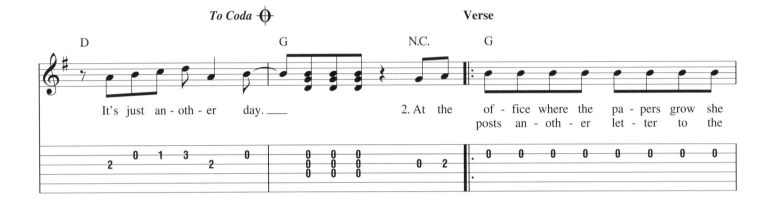

To Coda ⊕   **Verse**

It's just an - oth - er   day. ____   2. At the   of - fice where the   pa - pers grow   she
                                                          posts an - oth - er   let - ter to the

takes   a   break,   drinks an - oth - er   cof - fee, and   she   finds   it   hard   to   stay   a - wake. ____
sound   of   five,   peo - ple   gath - er   'round   her   and   she   finds   it   hard   to   stay   a - live. ____

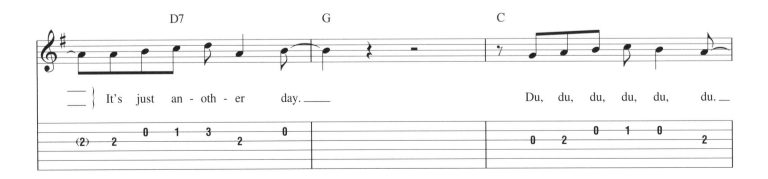

____ { It's   just   an - oth - er   day. ____   Du,   du,   du,   du,   du,   du. ____

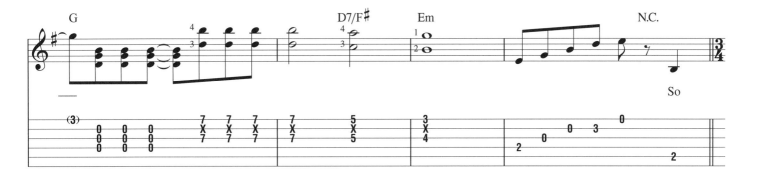

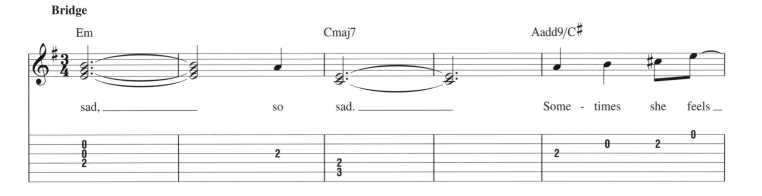

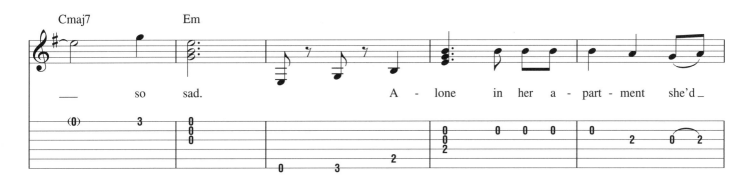

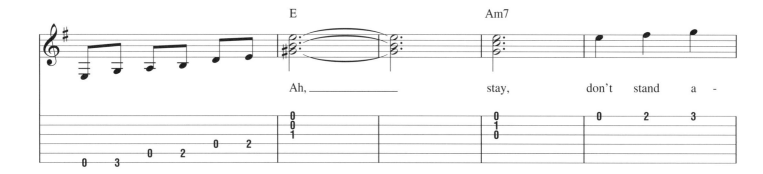

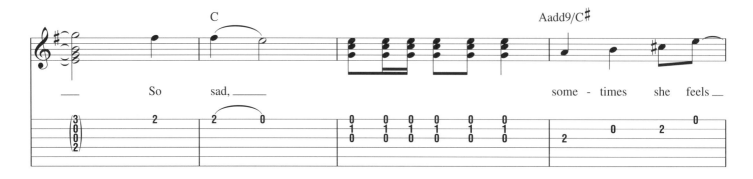

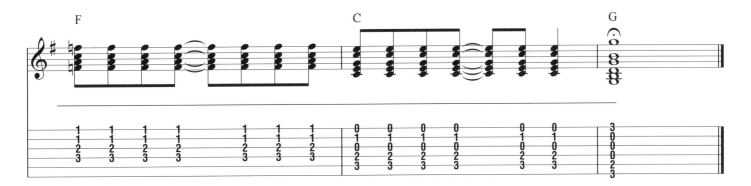

Silly Love Songs

Words and Music by Paul and Linda McCartney

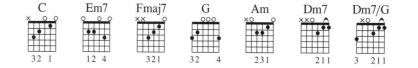

Strum Pattern: 6
Pick Pattern: 6

Intro
Moderately fast

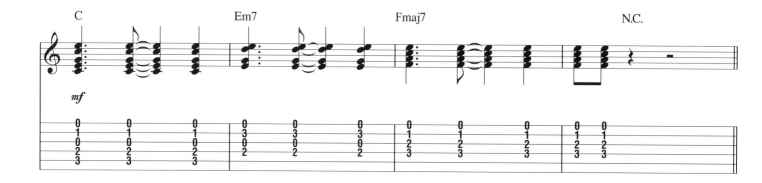

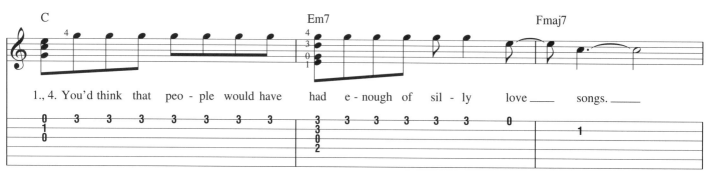

1., 4. You'd think that peo- ple would have had e- nough of sil- ly love ___ songs. ___

© 1976 (Renewed) MPL COMMUNICATIONS LTD.
Administered by MPL COMMUNICATIONS, INC.
All Rights Reserved

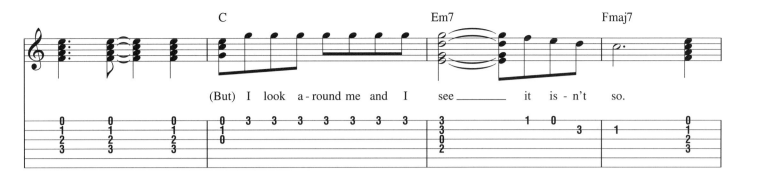

(But) I look a-round me and I see _____ it is-n't so.

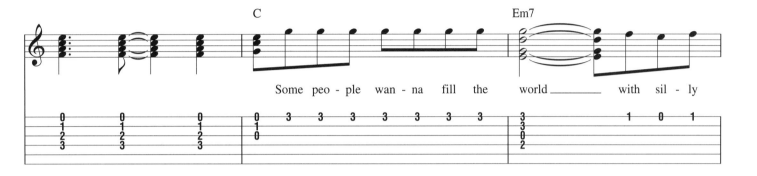

Some peo-ple wan-na fill the world _____ with sil-ly

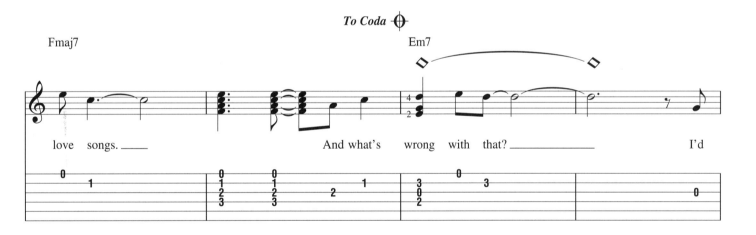

To Coda ⊕

love songs. _____ And what's wrong with that? _____ I'd

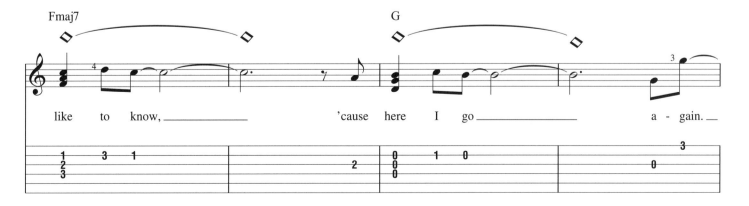

like to know, _____ 'cause here I go _____ a-gain. _____

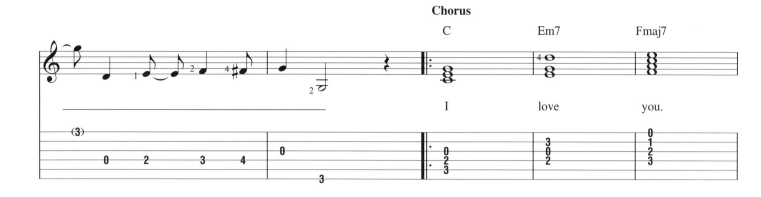

Chorus

I love you.

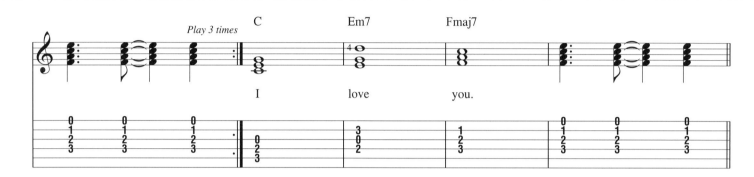

Play 3 times

I love you.

Verse

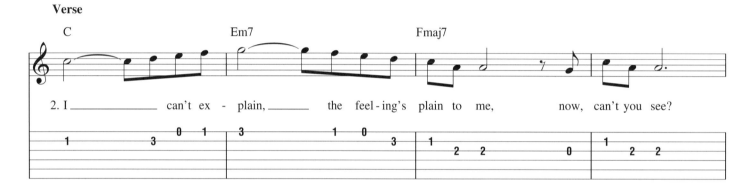

2. I _____ can't ex - plain, _____ the feel - ing's plain to me, _____ now, can't you see?

Ah, she gave me more, _____ she gave it all to me, _____ now, can't you see? What's

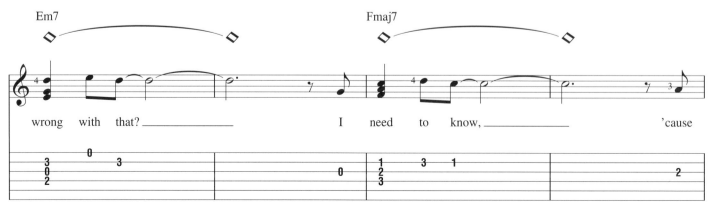

wrong with that? _____ I need to know, _____ 'cause

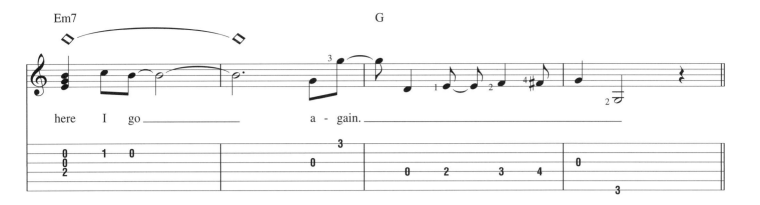

here I go _____ a - gain. _____

Chorus

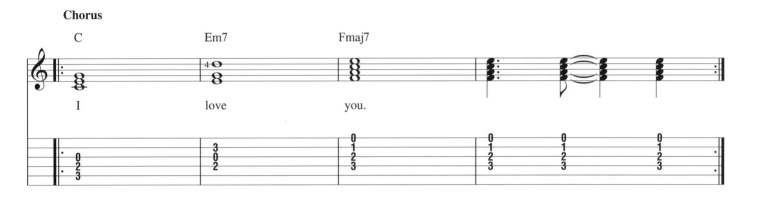

I love you.

Bridge

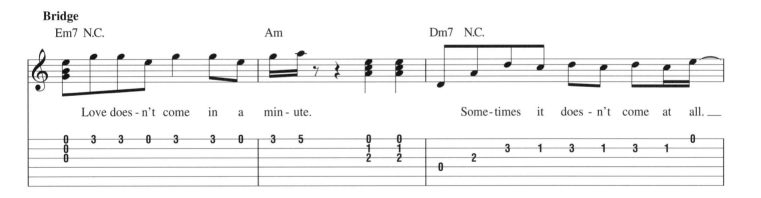

Love does-n't come in a min-ute. Some-times it does-n't come at all. ___

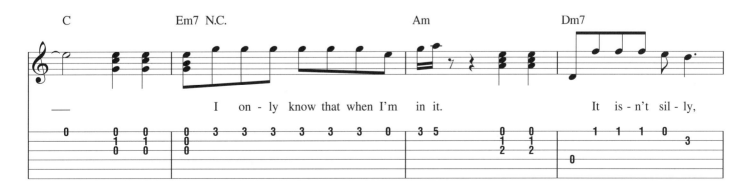

___ I on-ly know that when I'm in it. It is-n't sil-ly,

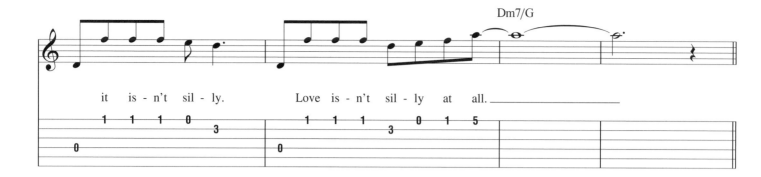

it is-n't sil-ly. Love is-n't sil-ly at all. _____

Interlude

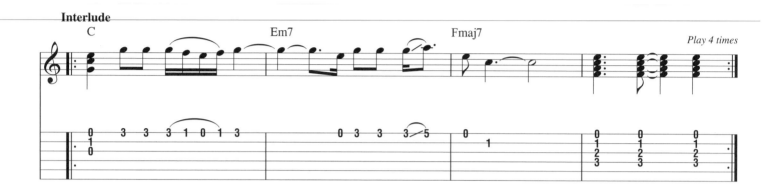

C   Em7   Fmaj7   *Play 4 times*

Verse

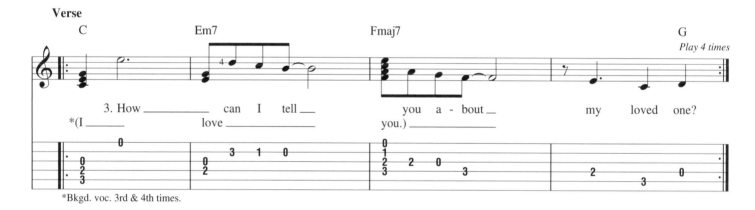

C   Em7   Fmaj7   G   *Play 4 times*

3. How _____ can I tell _____ you a - bout _____ my loved one?
*(I _____ love _____ you.) _____

*Bkgd. voc. 3rd & 4th times.

Interlude

C   Em7   Fmaj7   *Play 4 times*

Chorus

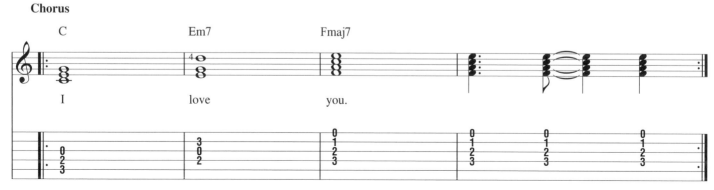

C   Em7   Fmaj7

I love you.

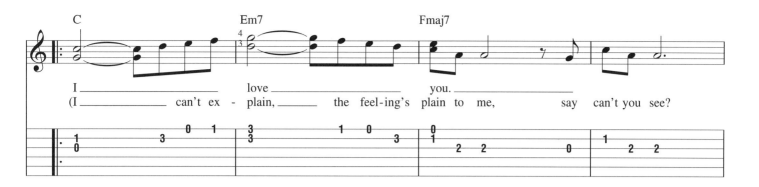

I _____ love _____ you. _____
(I _____ can't ex - plain, _____ the feel-ing's plain to me, _____ say can't you see?

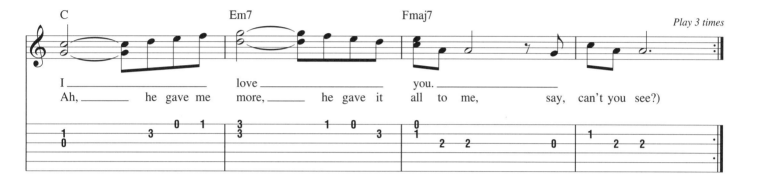

Play 3 times

I _____ love _____ you. _____
Ah, _____ he gave me _____ more, _____ he gave it _____ all to me, _____ say, can't you see?)

Interlude

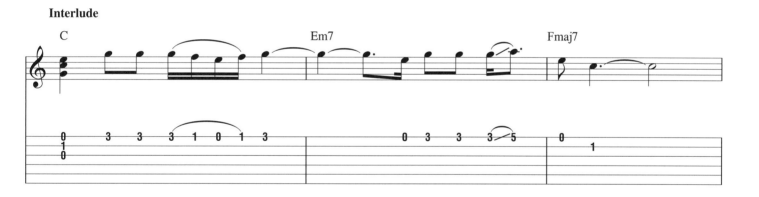

D.S. al Coda   **⊕ Coda**

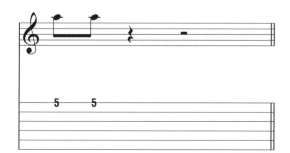

wrong with that? _____

Let 'Em In

Words and Music by Paul and Linda McCartney

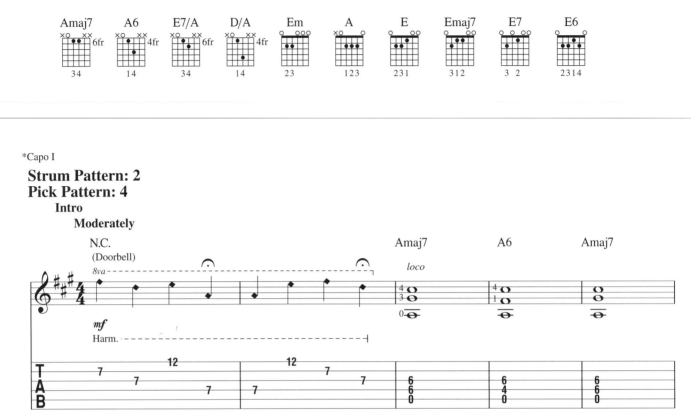

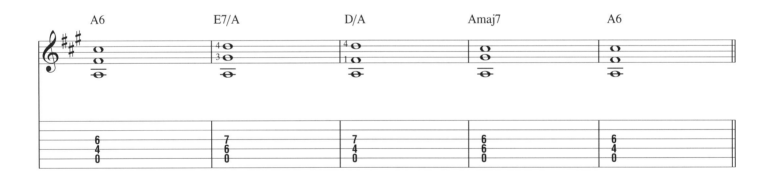

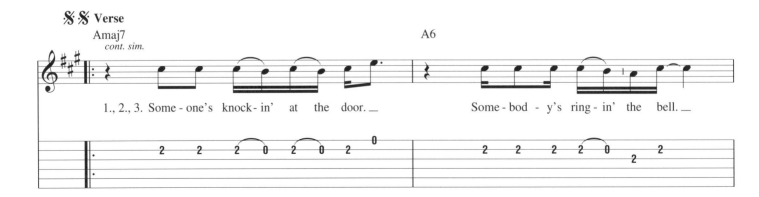

© 1976 (Renewed) MPL COMMUNICATIONS LTD.
Administered by MPL COMMUNICATIONS, INC.
All Rights Reserved

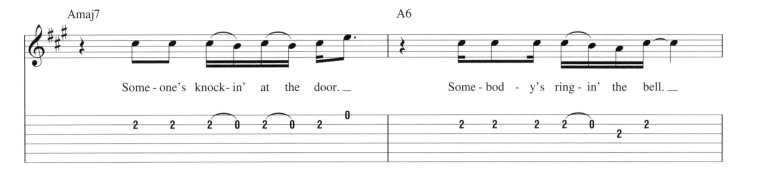

Some-one's knock-in' at the door. __

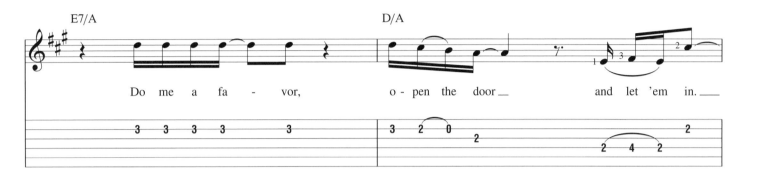

Some-bod - y's ring-in' the bell. __

Do me a fa - vor, o - pen the door __ and let 'em in. __

Interlude

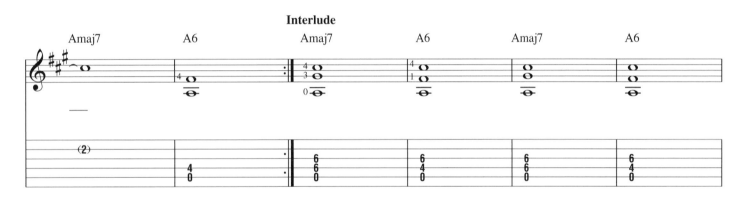

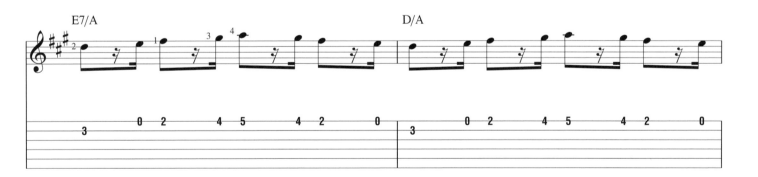

To Coda 2 ⊕

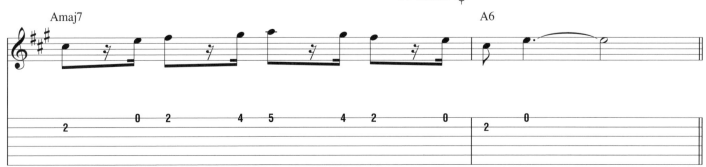

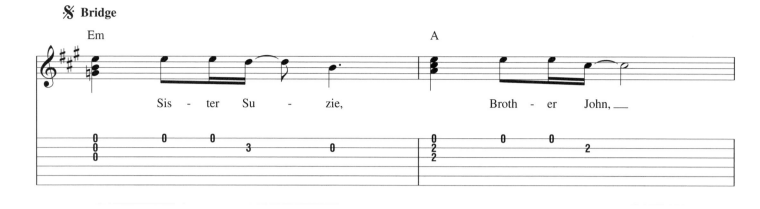

Sis - ter Su - zie, Broth - er John, ___

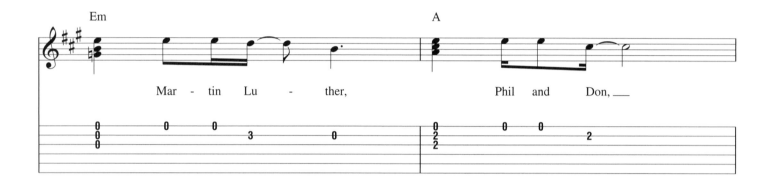

Mar - tin Lu - ther, Phil and Don, ___

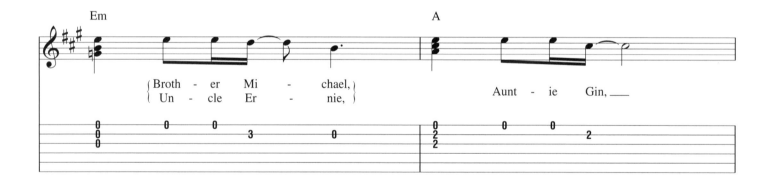

{ Broth - er Mi - chael, }
{ Un - cle Er - nie, } Aunt - ie Gin, ___

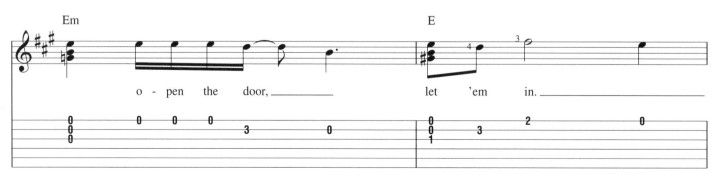

o - pen the door, ___ let 'em in. ___

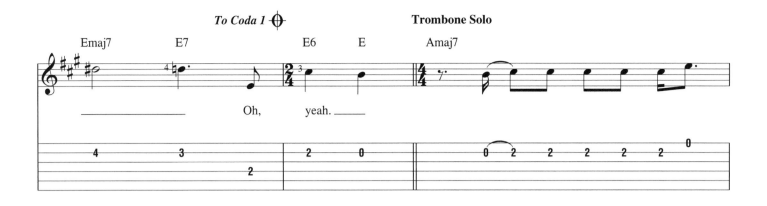

Oh,   yeah.

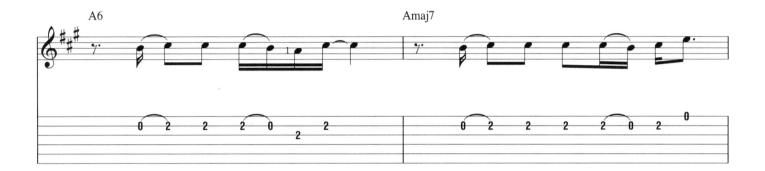

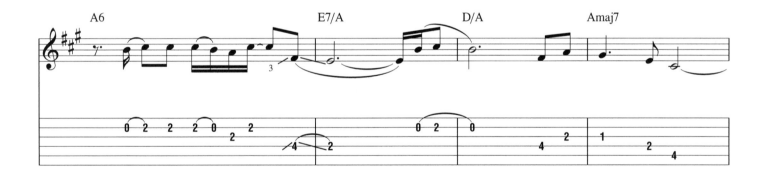

D.S. al Coda 1   ⊕ **Coda 1**   *D.S.S. al Coda 2*   ⊕ **Coda 2**
(no repeat)

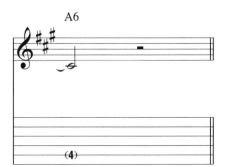

yeah.

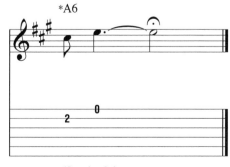

*Let chord ring.

Say Say Say

Words and Music by Paul McCartney and Michael Jackson

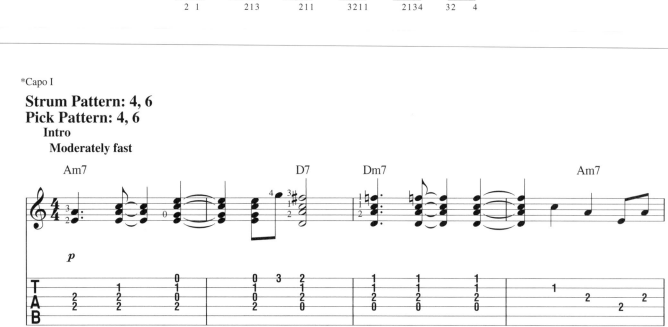

*Capo I

Strum Pattern: 4, 6
Pick Pattern: 4, 6

Intro

Moderately fast

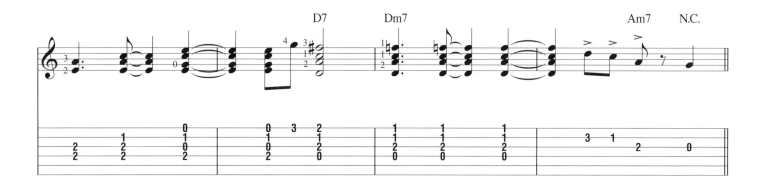

*Optional: To match recording, place capo at 1st fret.

Verse

Am7   D7   Dm7   Am7

1. Say,   say,— say ——— what you want,   but don't   play ——— games   with my af - fec - tion.
2., 3. *See additional lyrics*

© 1982, 1983 MPL COMMUNICATIONS, INC., WARNER-TAMERLANE PUBLISHING CORP. and MIJAC MUSIC
All Rights Reserved

Bridge

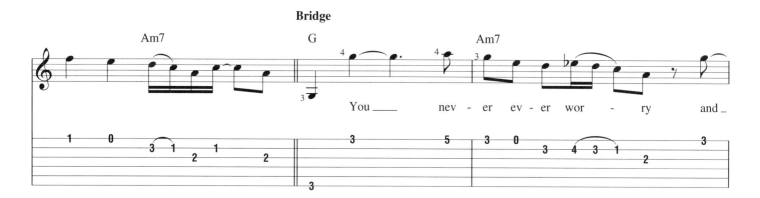

You _____ nev - er ev - er wor - ry and _

_ you nev - er shed a tear. _____ You're say - ing that my love _

D.S. al Coda

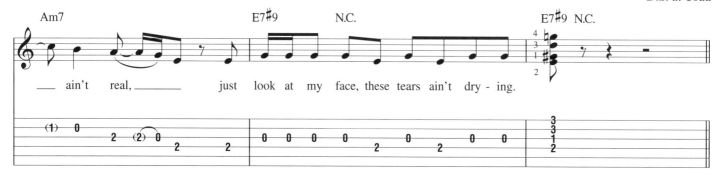

_ ain't real, _____ just look at my face, these tears ain't dry - ing.

Coda

Outro

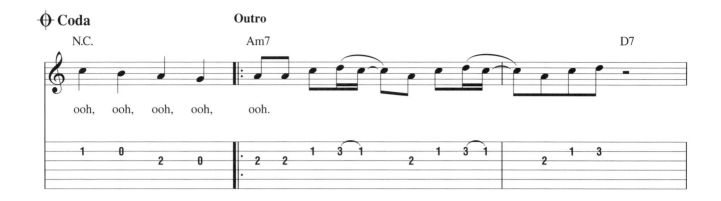

ooh, ooh, ooh, ooh, ooh.

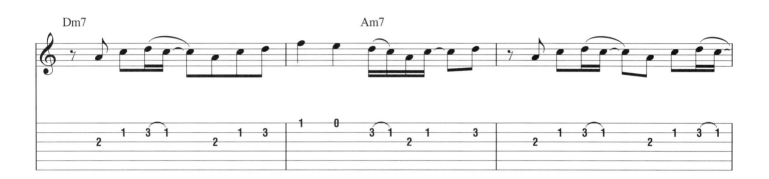

Repeat and fade

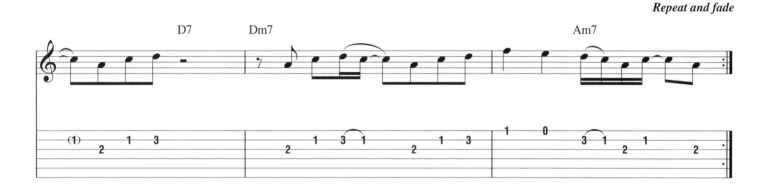

Additional Lyrics

2. Go, go, go where you want,
   But don't leave me here forever.
   You, you, you stay away
   So long girl, I see you never.

Chorus 2., 3. What can I do, girl, to get through to you?
   'Cause I love you, baby. (Baby.)
   Standing here baptized in all my tears.
   Baby, through the years, you know I'm crying
   Ooh, ooh, ooh, ooh, ooh.

3. You, you, you can never say
   That I'm not the one who really loves you.
   I pray, pray, pray, every day
   That you see things, girl, like I do.

Live and Let Die

Words and Music by Paul McCartney and Linda McCartney

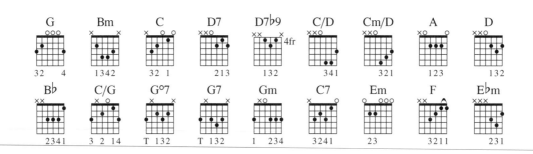

Strum Pattern: 5
Pick Pattern: 1

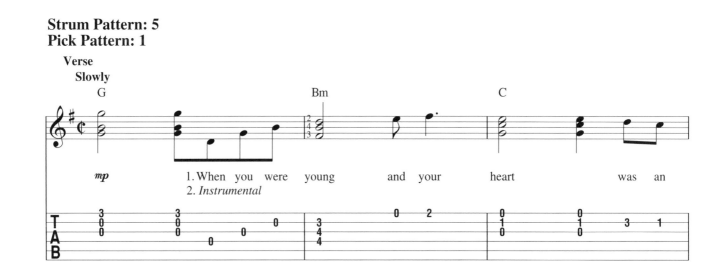

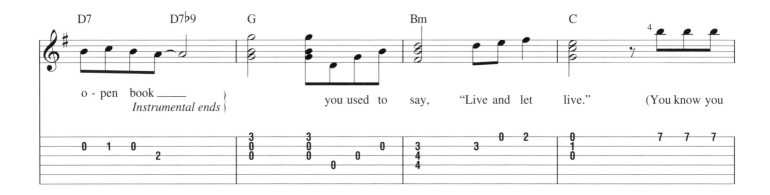

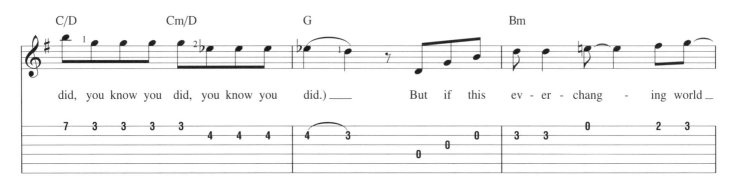

© 1973 (Renewed) PAUL and LINDA McCARTNEY and EMI UNART CATALOG INC.
All Rights for the U.S. and Canada Controlled by EMI UNART CATALOG INC.
All Rights Reserved   Used by Permission

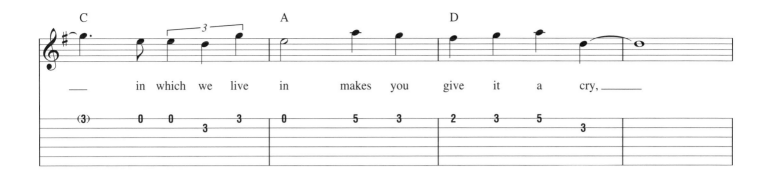

_____ in which we live in makes you give it a cry, _____

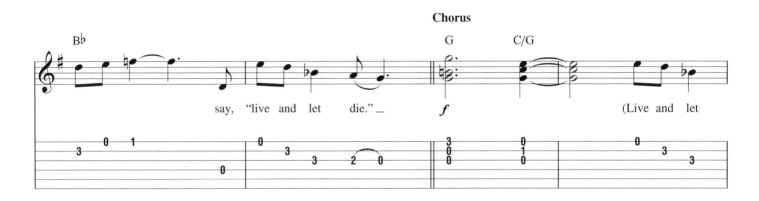

Chorus

say, "live and let die." _ (Live and let

die.) _____ Live and let die._____ (Live and let

Interlude

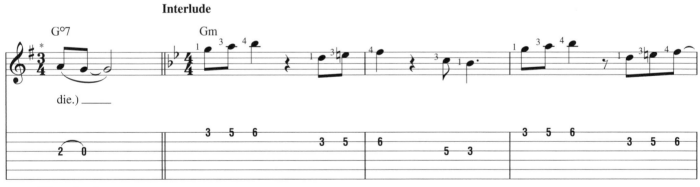

die.) _____

*Use pattern 8.

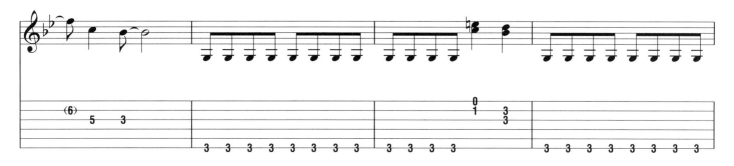

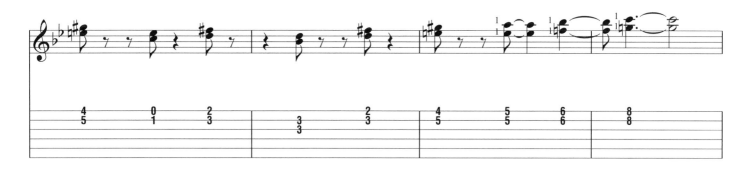

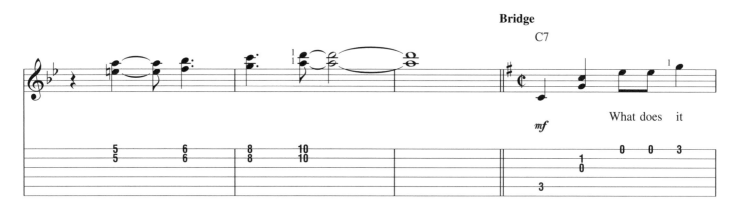

Bridge

What does it

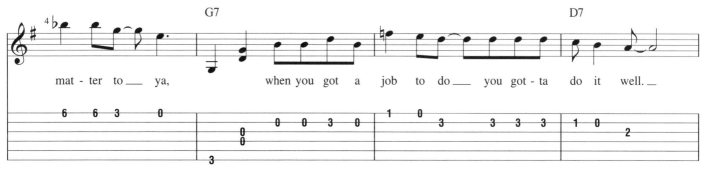

mat - ter to __ ya,   when you got a   job   to do __ you got - ta   do it   well. __

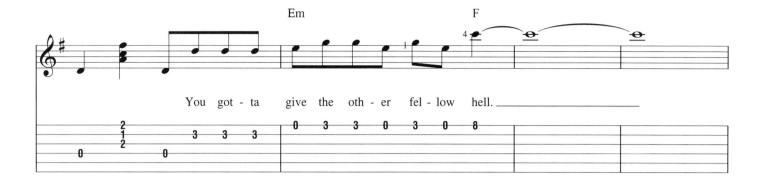

Em   F

You got-ta   give the oth-er fel-low hell. _____

Interlude

Gm

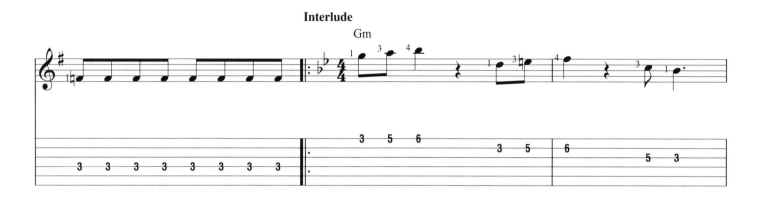

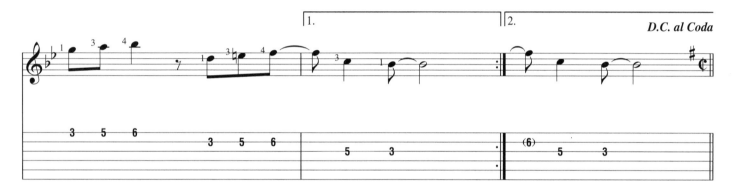

1.   2.   *D.C. al Coda*

⊕ Coda
Outro

Gm

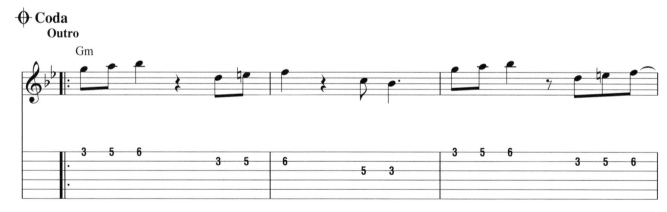

1.   2.   E♭m

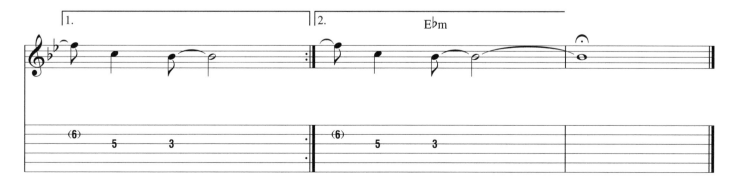

C Moon

Words and Music by Paul and Linda McCartney

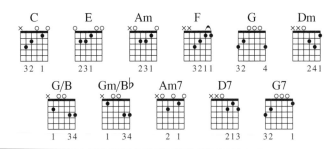

Strum Pattern: 3, 5
Pick Pattern: 5

Intro
    Moderate Reggae, in 2

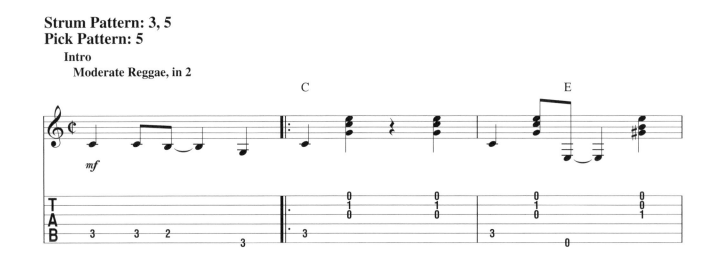

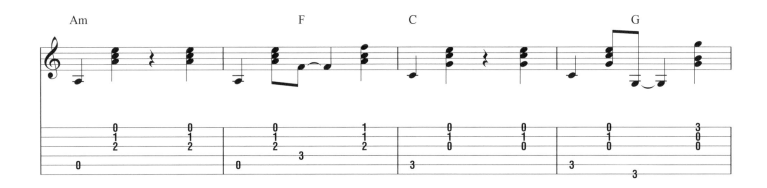

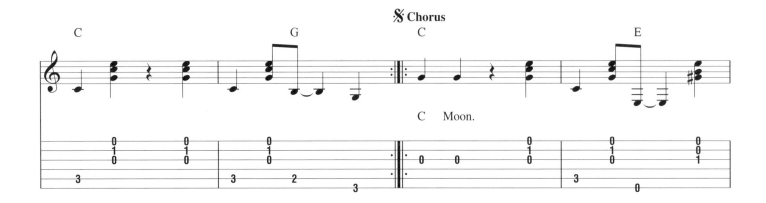

© 1973 (Renewed) PAUL and LINDA McCARTNEY
Administered by MPL COMMUNICATIONS, INC.
All Rights Reserved

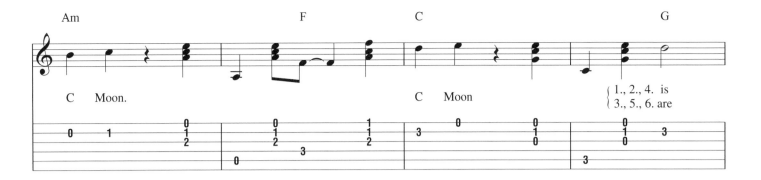

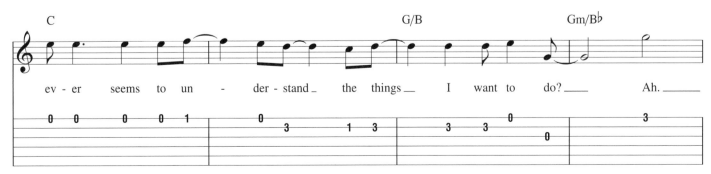

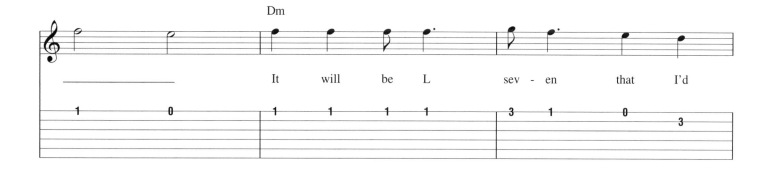

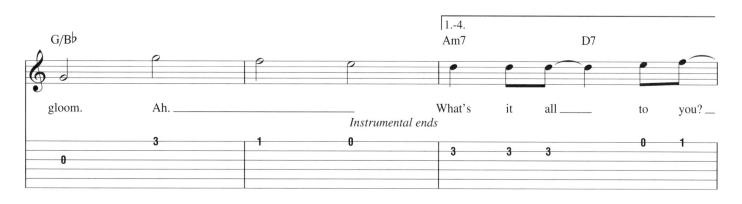

Additional Lyrics

2., 4. Bobby lived with Patty but they never told her daddy
What their love was all about. Ah.
She could tell a number that he thought up,
But she never was the type to let it out. Ah.
What's it all about?

Junior's Farm

Words and Music by Paul and Linda McCartney

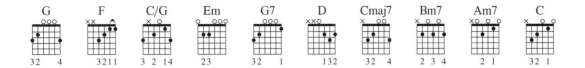

Strum Pattern: 1
Pick Pattern: 2

Intro
Moderately

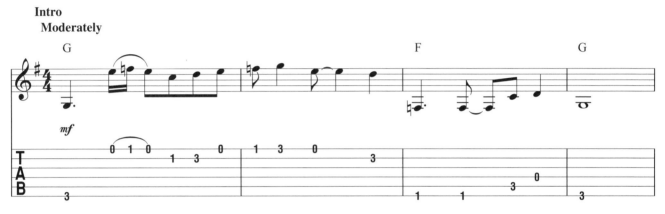

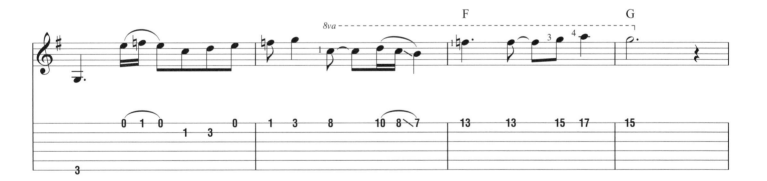

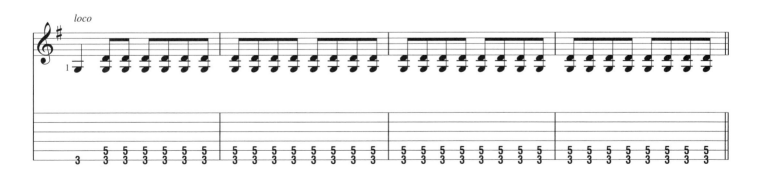

© 1974 (Renewed) PAUL and LINDA McCARTNEY
Administered by MPL COMMUNICATIONS, INC.
All Rights Reserved

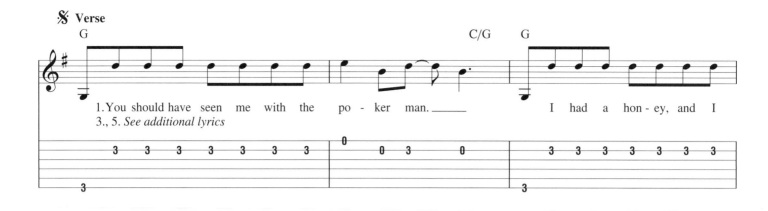

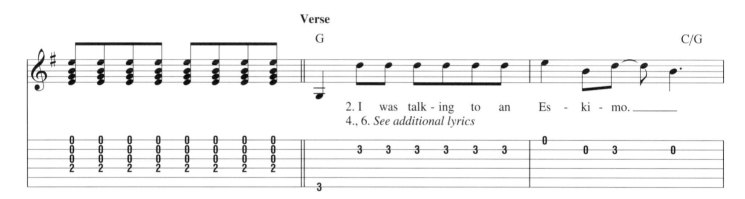

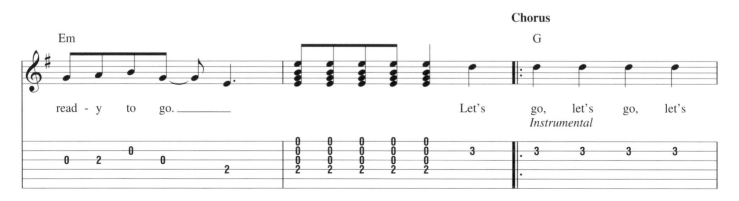

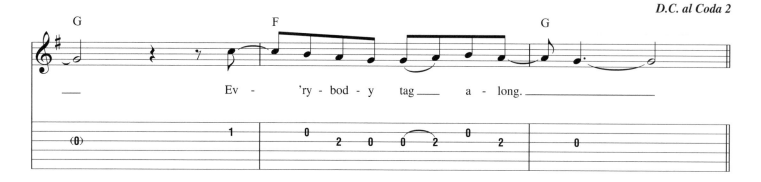

Ev - 'ry-bod - y tag ___ a - long. _____

 Coda 2

Let's go, let's go ___ down to Ju - nior's Farm where I

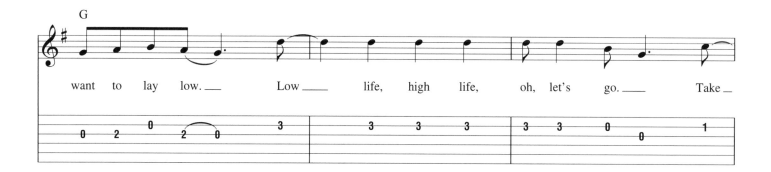

want to lay low. ___ Low ___ life, high life, oh, let's go. ___ Take _

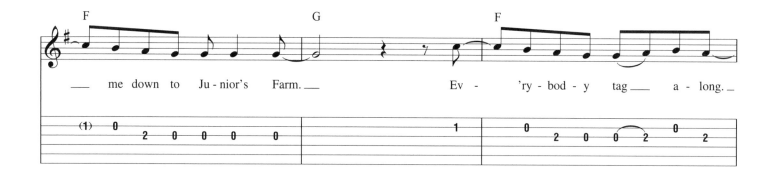

_ me down to Ju - nior's Farm. ___ Ev - 'ry-bod - y tag ___ a - long. _

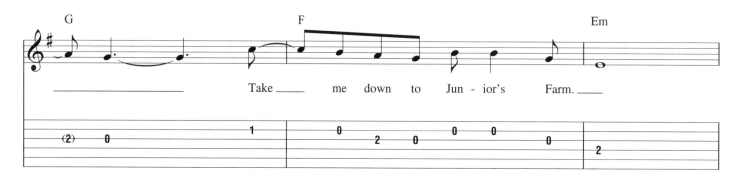

Take ___ me down to Jun - ior's Farm. ___

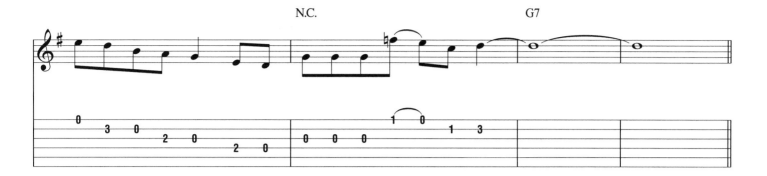

Outro

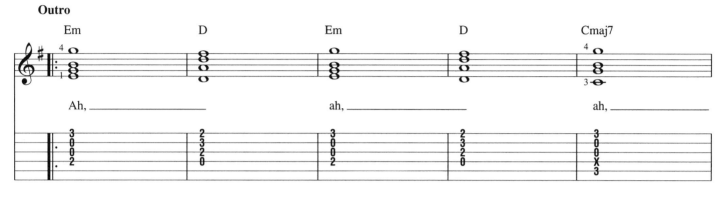

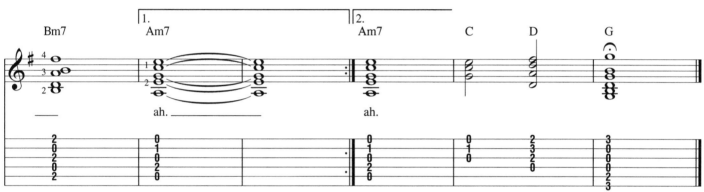

Additional Lyrics

3. At the Houses of Parliament
   Ev'rybody's talking 'bout the President.
   We all chip in for a bag of cement.

4. Ollie Hardy should have had more sense.
   He bought a geegee and he jumped the fence,
   All for the sake of a couple of pence.

5. I took my bag into a grocer's store.
   The price is higher than the time before.
   Old man asked me, "Why is it more?"

6. I said, "You should have seen me with the poker man.
   I had a honey, and I bet a grand.
   Just in the nick of time I looked at his hand."

Uncle Albert/Admiral Halsey

Words and Music by Paul and Linda McCartney

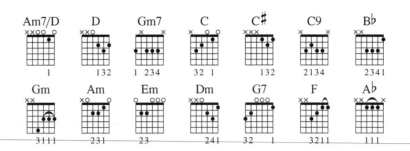

Strum Pattern: 1
Pick Pattern: 5

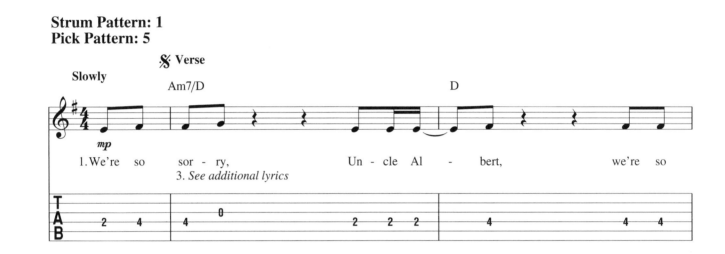

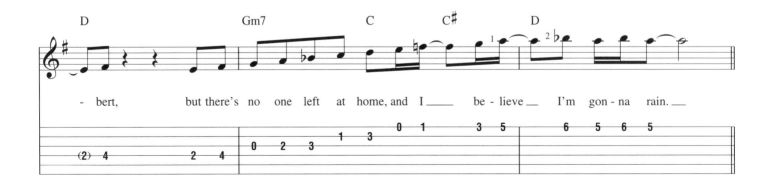

© 1971 (Renewed) PAUL and LINDA McCARTNEY
Administered by MPL COMMUNICATIONS, INC.
All Rights Reserved

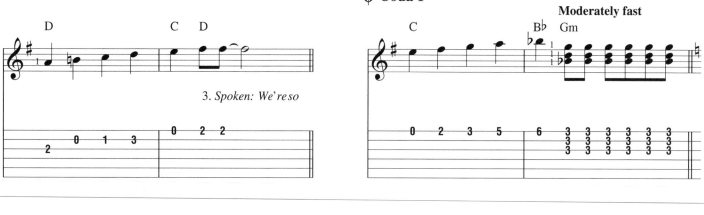

3. *Spoken: We're so*

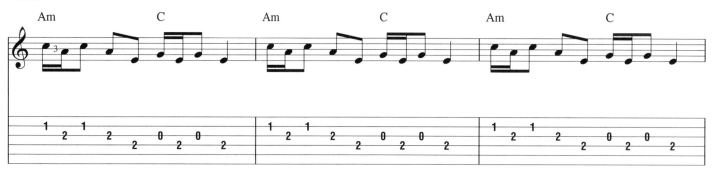

Interlude

Bridge

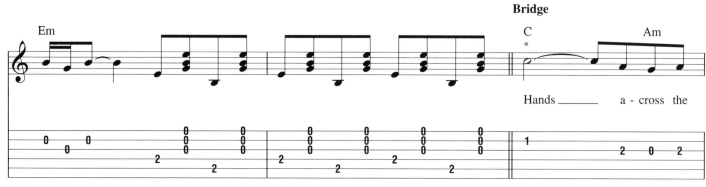

Hands _____ a - cross the

*Sung one octave higher till end.

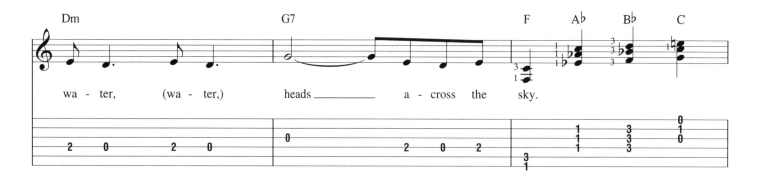

wa - ter, (wa - ter,) heads _____ a - cross the sky.

To Coda 2 ⊕

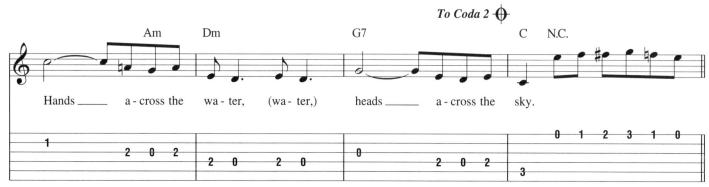

Hands _____ a - cross the wa - ter, (wa - ter,) heads _____ a - cross the sky.

Verse

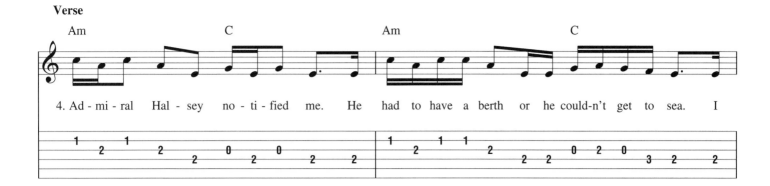

4. Ad - mi - ral Hal - sey no - ti - fied me. He had to have a berth or he could-n't get to sea. I

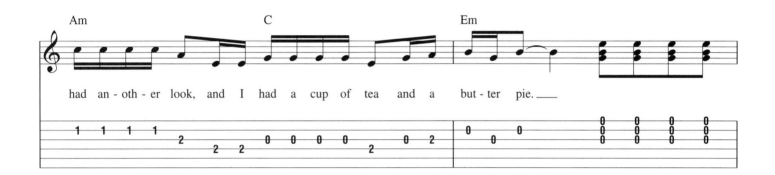

had an - oth - er look, and I had a cup of tea and a but - ter pie. ___

Bridge

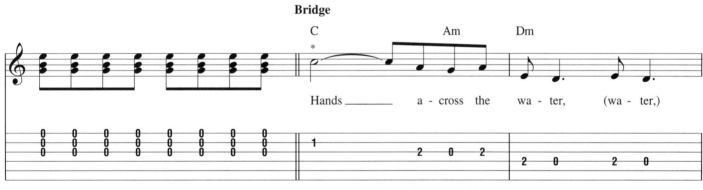

Hands ___ a - cross the wa - ter, (wa - ter,)

*Sung one octave higher throughout Bridge.

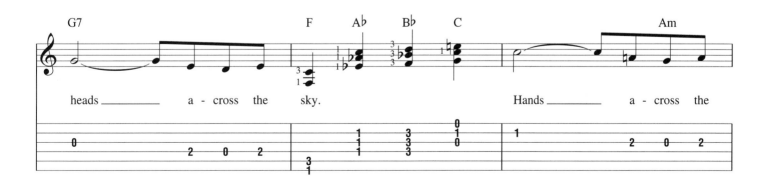

heads ___ a - cross the sky. Hands ___ a - cross the

wa - ter, (wa - ter,) heads _____ a - cross the sky.

Verse

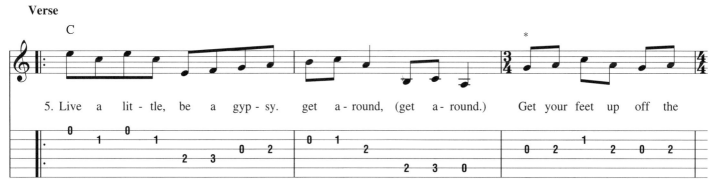

5. Live a lit - tle, be a gyp - sy. get a - round, (get a - round.) Get your feet up off the

*Use Pattern 9.

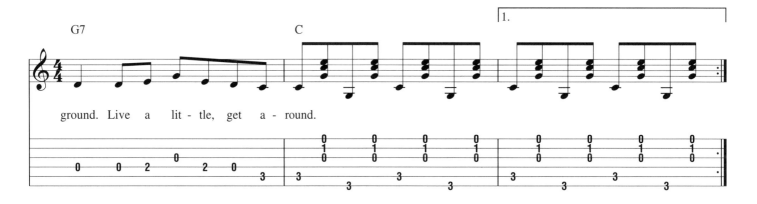

ground. Live a lit - tle, get a - round.

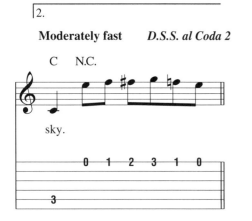

Moderately fast   *D.S.S. al Coda 2*

sky.

⊕ **Coda 2**

Faster

Repeat and fade

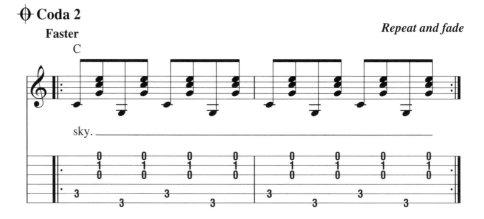

sky. _____

Additional Lyrics

3. *Spoken: We're so sorry, Uncle Albert,*
   But we haven't done a bloody thing all day.
   We're so sorry, Uncle Albert,
   But the kettle's on the boil
   And we're so easily called away.

My Love

Words and Music by Paul and Linda McCartney

*Capo III

Strum Pattern: 4
Pick Pattern: 5

Verse
Slowly, in 2

1. And when I go a-way, ___ I know my
2., 4. *See additional lyrics*
3. *Instrumental*

*Optional: To match recording, place capo at 3rd fret.

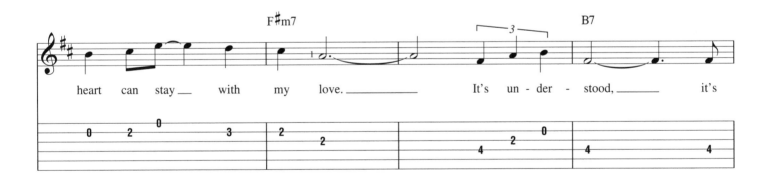

heart can stay ___ with my love. ___ It's un-der-stood, ___ it's

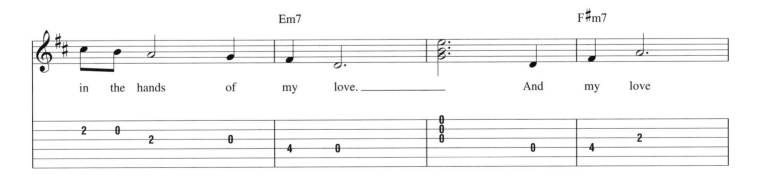

in the hands of my love. ___ And my love

© 1973 (Renewed) PAUL and LINDA McCARTNEY
Administered by MPL COMMUNICATIONS, INC.
All Rights Reserved

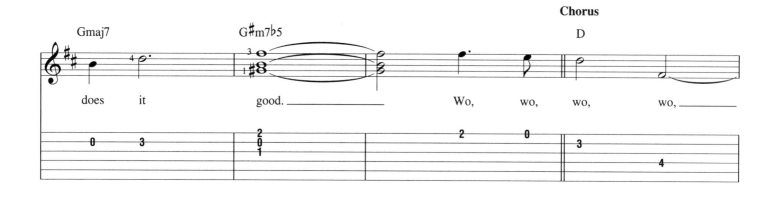

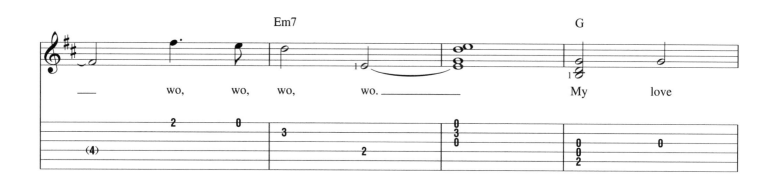

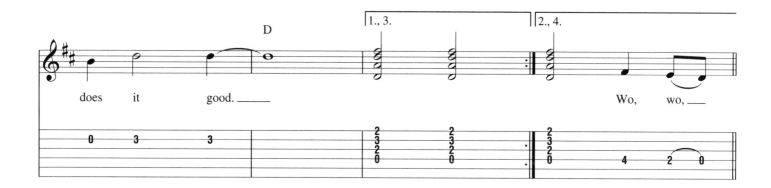

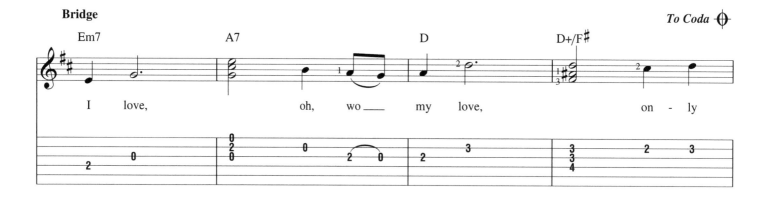

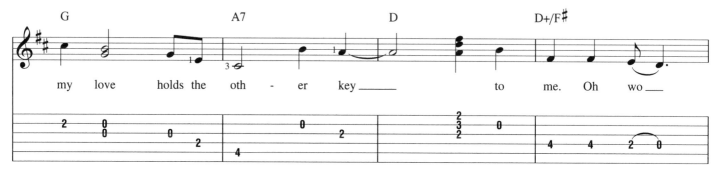

D.C. al Coda
(take repeat)

Coda

Freely

Outro
A tempo

my love does it good to _____ me.

Wo, wo, wo, wo, wo, _____ wo, _____ wo.

Additional Lyrics

2. And when the cupboard's bare,
   I'll still find something there with my love.
   It's understood, it's everywhere with my love.
   And my love does it good.

4. Don't ever ask me why
   I can never say goodbye to my love.
   It's understood, it's everywhere with my love.
   And my love does it good.

Coming Up

Words and Music by Paul McCartney

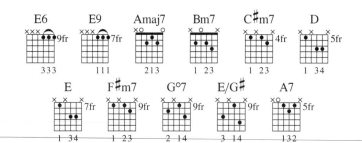

Strum Pattern: 1
Pick Pattern: 5

Intro
Moderately

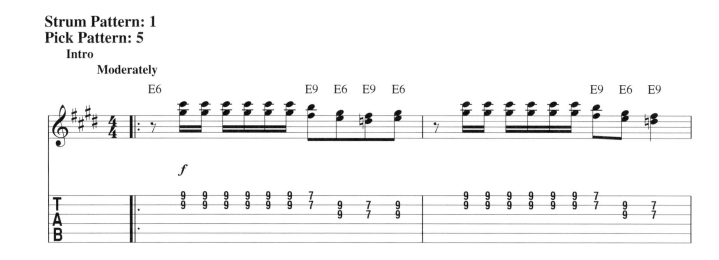

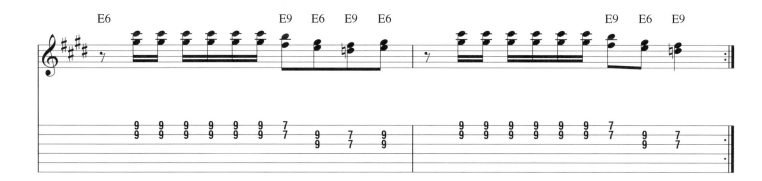

𝄋 Verse

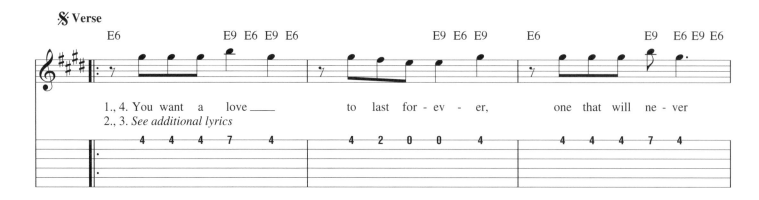

1., 4. You want a love ____ to last for-ev-er, one that will ne-ver
2., 3. *See additional lyrics*

© 1980 MPL COMMUNICATIONS LTD.
Administered by MPL COMMUNICATIONS, INC.
All Rights Reserved

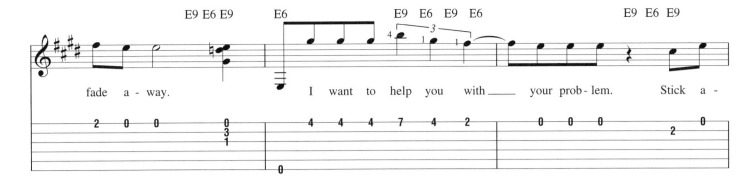

fade a - way.   I want to help you with ___ your prob - lem.   Stick a -

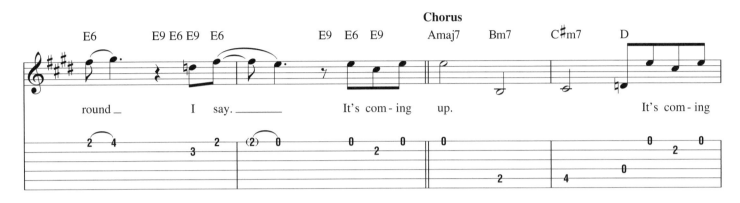

Chorus

round ___   I say. _____   It's com - ing   up.   It's com - ing

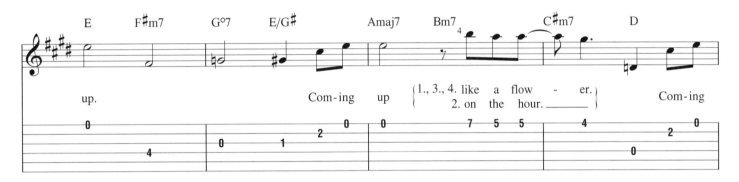

up.   Com-ing   up   { 1., 3., 4. like a flow - er. }   Com-ing
                                       { 2. on   the hour. _____ }

To Coda 2 ⊕   *To Coda 1* ⊕

Interlude

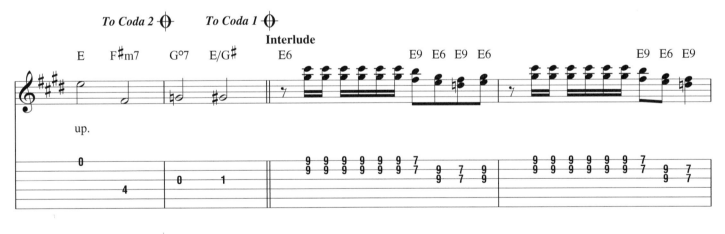

up.

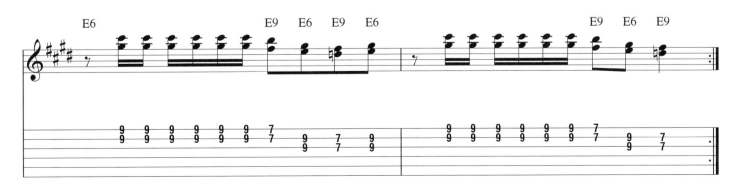

Bridge

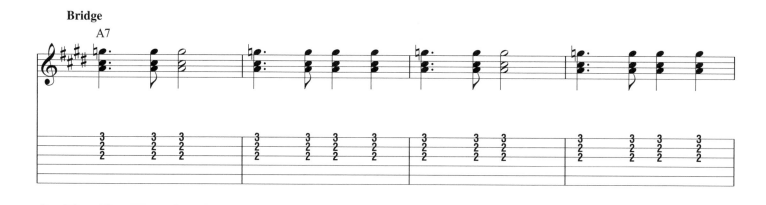

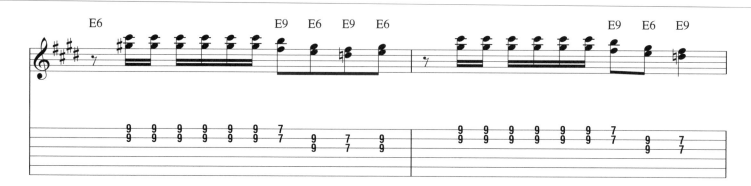

D.S. al Coda 1

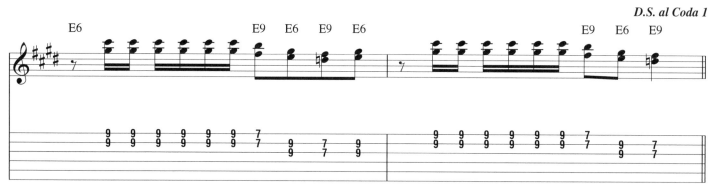

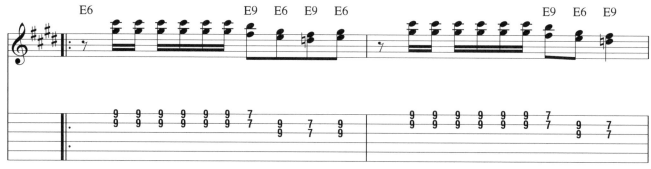

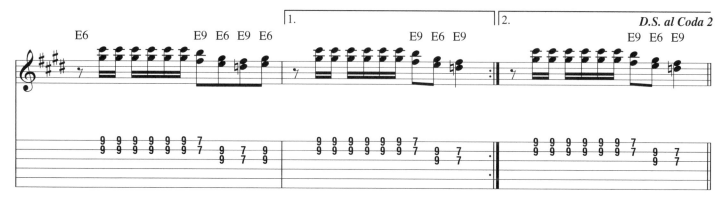

⊕ Coda 2

Outro-Chorus

Additional Lyrics

2. You want a friend you can rely on.
One who will never fade away.
And if you're searching for an answer,
Stick around I say.

3. You want a better kind of future.
One that everyone can share.
You're not alone, we all could use it.
Stick around, we're nearly there.

Goodnight Tonight

Words and Music by Paul McCartney

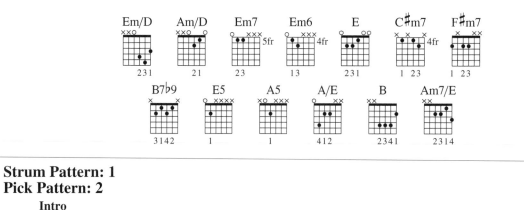

Strum Pattern: 1
Pick Pattern: 2

Intro
Moderately

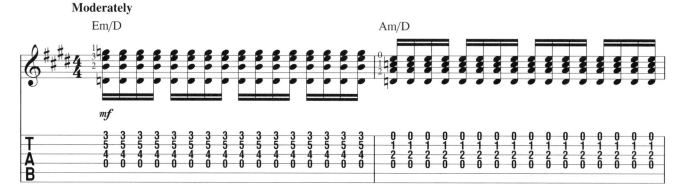

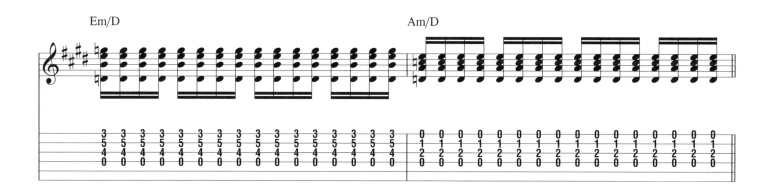

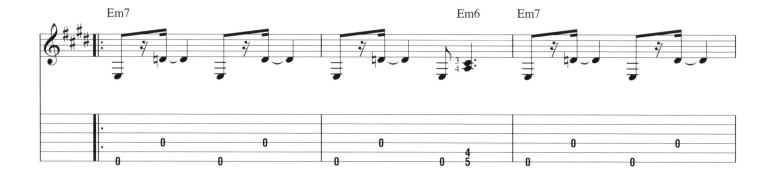

© 1979 MPL COMMUNICATIONS LTD.
Administered by MPL COMMUNICATIONS, INC.
All Rights Reserved

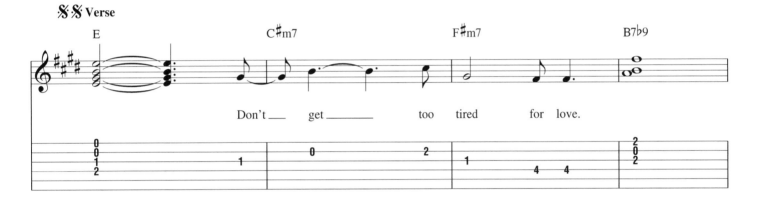

Don't get too tired for love.

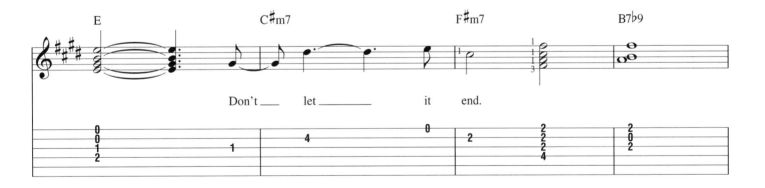

Don't let it end.

Don't say good-night to love.

It
It's

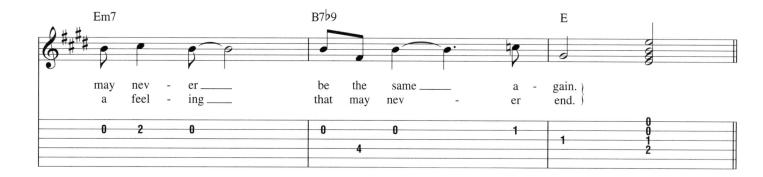

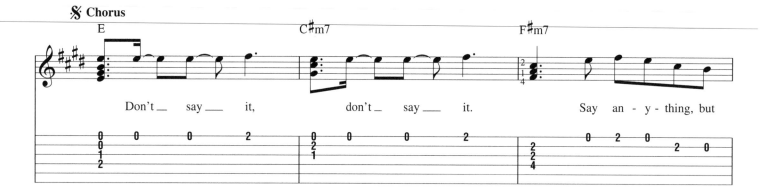

Chorus

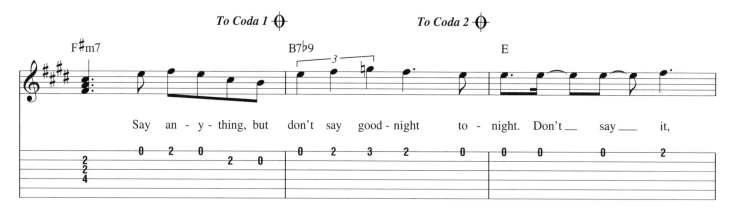

To Coda 1 ⊕   *To Coda 2* ⊕

Interlude

*Sung 1st time only.

Guitar Solo

D.S. al Coda 1

Coda 1

don't say good - night to - night.

*Let chord ring.

Interlude

Guitar Solo

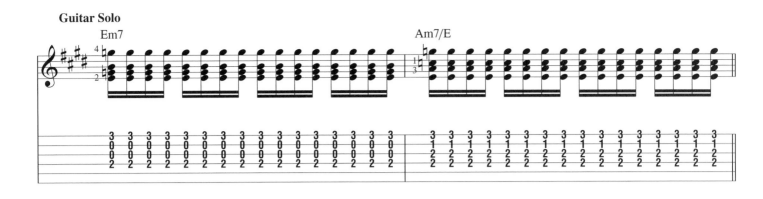

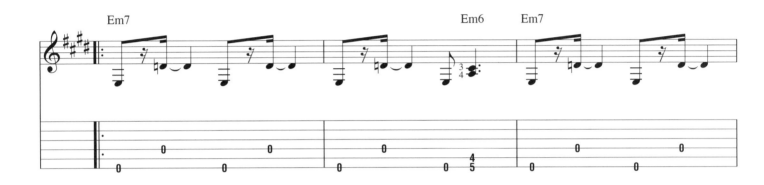

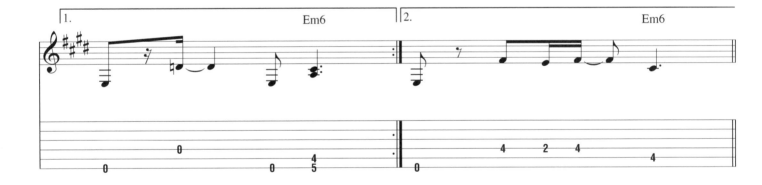

Interlude

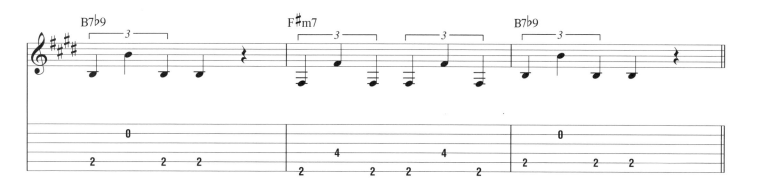

2nd time, D.S.S. al Coda 2

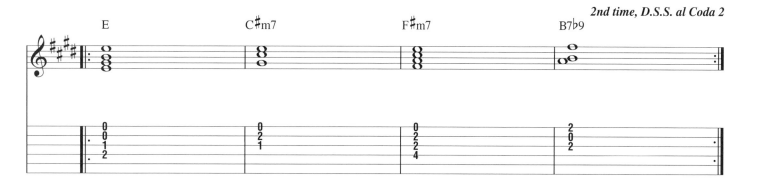

⊕ Coda 2

Outro-Chorus

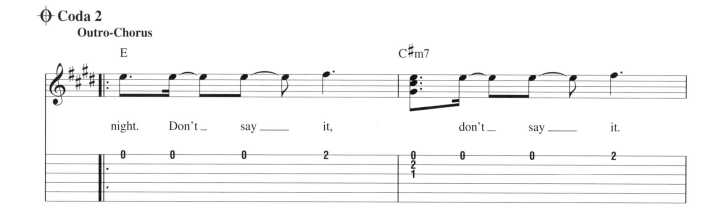

night. Don't _ say _____ it, don't _ say _____ it.

Repeat and fade

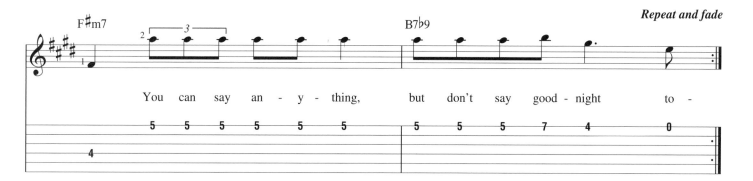

You can say an - y - thing, but don't say good - night to -

With a Little Luck

Words and Music by Paul McCartney

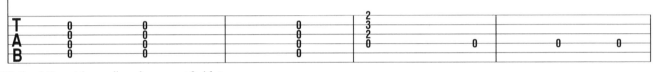

*Capo II

**Strum Pattern: 6

**Pick Pattern: 3

Intro
Moderately

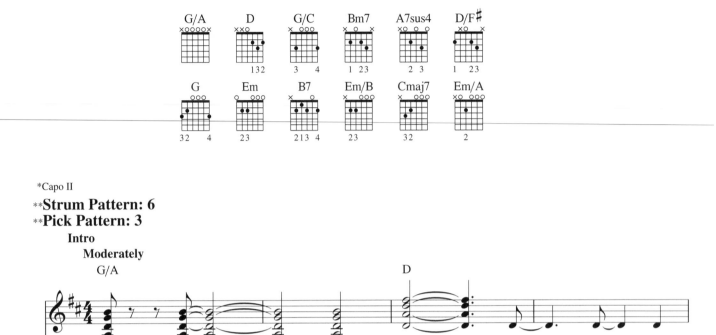

*Optional: To match recording, place capo at 2nd fret.

**Use Pattern 10 for $\frac{2}{4}$ measures.

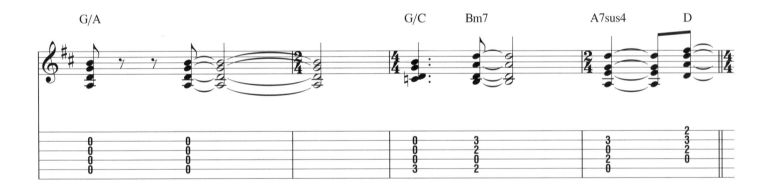

1. With a lit-tle luck,___ we can help it out.___ We can make this whole___
2., 3. *See additional lyrics*

© 1978 MPL COMMUNICATIONS, INC.
All Rights Reserved

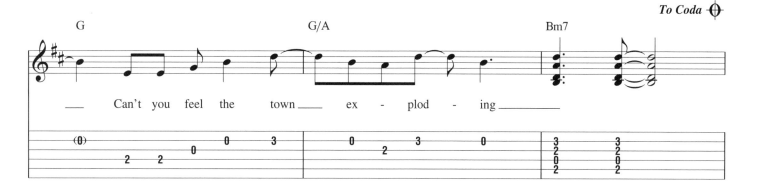

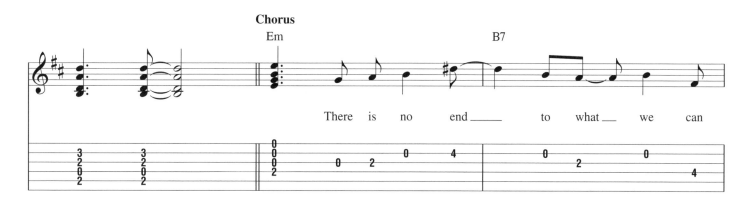

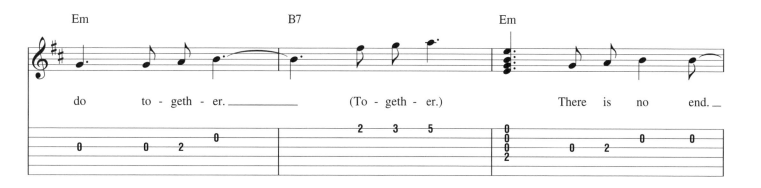

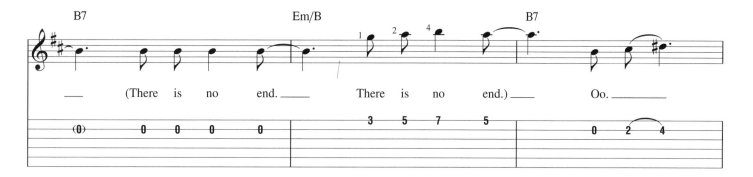

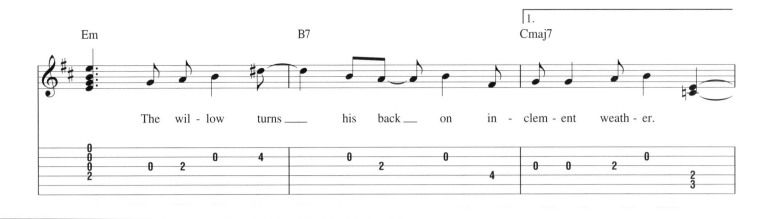

The wil - low turns ___ his back ___ on in - clem - ent weath - er.

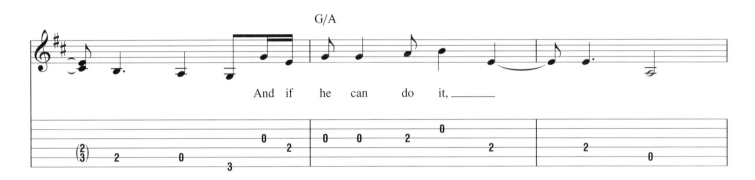

And if he can do it, ___

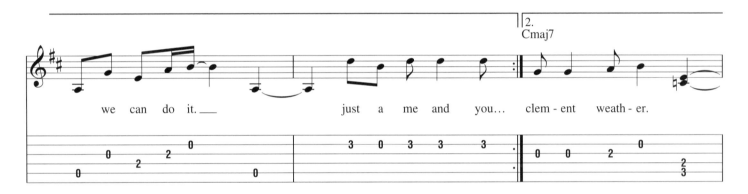

we can do it. ___ just a me and you... clem - ent weath - er.

D.S. al Coda

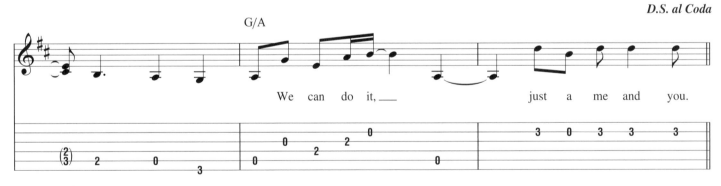

We can do it, ___ just a me and you.

 Coda

Outro-Verse

With a lit - tle luck. With a lit - tle luck. With a

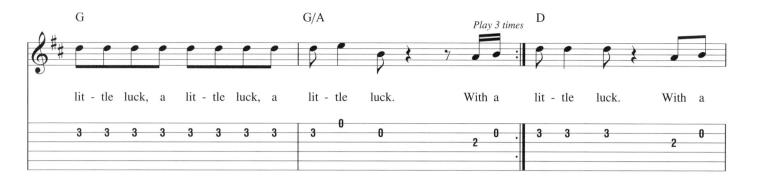

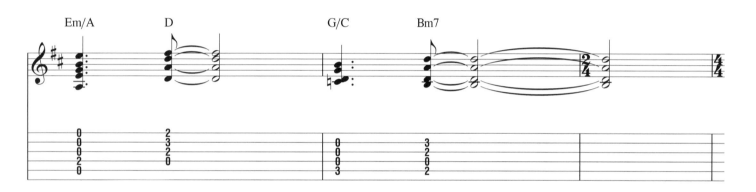

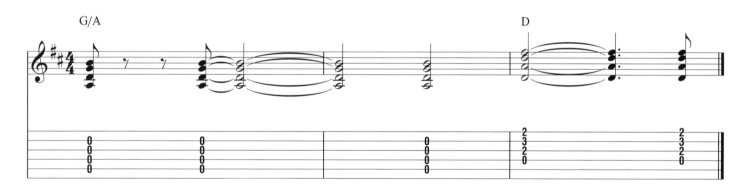

Additional Lyrics

2. And a little luck, we can clear it up.
   We can bring it in for a landing,
   With a little luck, we can turn it on.
   There can be no misunderstanding.

3. With a little push, we could set it off.
   We could send it rocketing skywards.
   With a little love, we could shake it up.
   Don't you feel the comet exploding?

EASY GUITAR
WITH NOTES & TAB

This series features simplified arrangements with notes, tab, chord charts, and strum and pick patterns.

MIXED FOLIOS

00702002	Acoustic Rock Hits for Easy Guitar	$12.95
00702166	All-Time Best Guitar Collection	$17.95
00699665	Beatles Best	$12.95
00702232	Best Acoustic Songs for Easy Guitar	$12.99
00702233	Best Hard Rock Songs	$14.99
00698978	Big Christmas Collection	$16.95
00702115	Blues Classics	$10.95
00385020	Broadway Songs for Kids	$9.95
00702237	Christian Acoustic Favorites	$12.95
00702149	Children's Christian Songbook	$7.95
00702028	Christmas Classics	$7.95
00702185	Christmas Hits	$9.95
00702016	Classic Blues for Easy Guitar	$12.95
00702141	Classic Rock	$8.95
00702203	CMT's 100 Greatest Country Songs	$27.95
00702170	Contemporary Christian Christmas	$9.95
00702006	Contemporary Christian Favorites	$9.95
00702065	Contemporary Women of Country	$9.95
00702121	Country from the Heart	$9.95
00702240	Country Hits of 2007-2008	$12.95
00702225	Country Hits of '06-'07	$12.95
00702085	Disney Movie Hits	$12.95
00702257	Easy Acoustic Guitar Songs	$14.99
00702212	Essential Christmas	$9.95
00702041	Favorite Hymns for Easy Guitar	$9.95
00702174	God Bless America® & Other Songs for a Better Nation	$8.95
00699374	Gospel Favorites	$14.95
00702160	The Great American Country Songbook	$12.95
00702050	Great Classical Themes for Easy Guitar	$6.95
00702131	Great Country Hits of the '90s	$8.95
00702116	Greatest Hymns for Guitar	$8.95
00702130	The Groovy Years	$9.95
00702184	Guitar Instrumentals	$9.95
00702231	High School Musical for Easy Guitar	$12.95
00702241	High School Musical 2	$12.95
00702249	High School Musical 3	$12.99
00702037	Hits of the '50s for Easy Guitar	$10.95
00702046	Hits of the '70s for Easy Guitar	$8.95
00702047	Hits of the '80s for Easy Guitar	$9.95
00702032	International Songs for Easy Guitar	$12.95
00702051	Jock Rock for Easy Guitar	$9.95
00702162	Jumbo Easy Guitar Songbook	$19.95
00702112	Latin Favorites	$9.95
00702258	Legends of Rock	$14.99
00702138	Mellow Rock Hits	$10.95
00702147	Motown's Greatest Hits	$9.95
00702114	Movie Love Songs	$9.95
00702039	Movie Themes	$10.95
00702210	Best of MTV Unplugged	$12.95
00702189	MTV's 100 Greatest Pop Songs	$24.95
00702187	Selections from *O Brother Where Art Thou?*	$12.95
00702178	100 Songs for Kids	$12.95
00702158	Songs from Passion	$9.95
00702125	Praise and Worship for Guitar	$9.95
00702155	Rock Hits for Guitar	$9.95
00702242	Rock Band	$19.95
00702256	Rock Band 2	$19.99
00702128	Rockin' Down the Highway	$9.95
00702207	Smash Hits for Guitar	$9.95
00702110	The Sound of Music	$9.99
00702124	Today's Christian Rock – 2nd Edition	$9.95
00702220	Today's Country Hits	$9.95
00702198	Today's Hits for Guitar	$9.95
00702217	Top Christian Hits	$12.95
00702235	Top Christian Hits of '07-'08	$14.95
00702246	Top Hits of 2008	$12.95
00702206	Very Best of Rock	$9.95
00702175	VH1's 100 Greatest Songs of Rock and Roll	$24.95
00702192	Worship Favorites	$9.95

ARTIST COLLECTIONS

00702001	Best of Aerosmith	$16.95
00702040	Best of the Allman Brothers	$12.95
00702169	Best of The Beach Boys	$10.95
00702201	The Essential Black Sabbath	$12.95
00702140	Best of Brooks & Dunn	$10.95
00702095	Best of Mariah Carey	$12.95
00702043	Best of Johnny Cash	$12.95
00702033	Best of Steven Curtis Chapman	$14.95
00702073	Steven Curtis Chapman – Favorites	$10.95
00702090	Eric Clapton's Best	$10.95
00702086	Eric Clapton – from the Album *Unplugged*	$10.95
00702202	The Essential Eric Clapton	$12.95
00702250	blink-182 – Greatest Hits	$12.99
00702053	Best of Patsy Cline	$10.95
00702229	The Very Best of Creedence Clearwater Revival	$12.95
00702145	Best of Jim Croce	$10.95
00702219	David Crowder*Band Collection	$12.95
00702122	The Doors for Easy Guitar	$12.99
00702099	Best of Amy Grant	$9.95
00702190	Best of Pat Green	$19.95
00702136	Best of Merle Haggard	$10.95
00702243	Hannah Montana	$14.95
00702244	Hannah Montana 2/Meet Miley Cyrus	$16.95
00702227	Jimi Hendrix – Smash Hits	$14.99
00702236	Best of Antonio Carlos Jobim	$12.95
00702087	Best of Billy Joel	$10.95
00702245	Elton John – Greatest Hits 1970-2002	$14.99
00702204	Robert Johnson	$9.95
00702199	Norah Jones – Come Away with Me	$10.95
00702234	Selections from Toby Keith – 35 Biggest Hits	$12.95
00702003	Kiss	$9.95
00702193	Best of Jennifer Knapp	$12.95
00702097	John Lennon – Imagine	$9.95
00702216	Lynyrd Skynyrd	$14.95
00702182	The Essential Bob Marley	$12.95
00702129	Songs of Sarah McLachlan	$12.95
02501316	Metallica – Death Magnetic	$15.95
00702209	Steve Miller Band – Young Hearts (Greatest Hits)	$12.95
00702096	Best of Nirvana	$14.95
00702211	The Offspring – Greatest Hits	$12.95
00702030	Best of Roy Orbison	$12.95
00702144	Best of Ozzy Osbourne	$12.95
00702139	Elvis Country Favorites	$9.95
00699415	Best of Queen for Guitar	$14.99
00702208	Red Hot Chili Peppers – Greatest Hits	$12.95
00702093	Rolling Stones Collection	$17.95
00702092	Best of the Rolling Stones	$14.99
00702196	Best of Bob Seger	$12.95
00702252	Frank Sinatra – Nothing But the Best	$12.99
00702010	Best of Rod Stewart	$14.95
00702150	Best of Sting	$12.95
00702049	Best of George Strait	$12.95
00702259	Taylor Swift for Easy Guitar	$12.99
00702223	Chris Tomlin – Arriving	$12.95
00702226	Chris Tomlin – See the Morning	$12.95
00702132	Shania Twain – Greatest Hits	$10.95
00702108	Best of Stevie Ray Vaughan	$10.95
00702123	Best of Hank Williams	$9.95
00702111	Stevie Wonder – Guitar Collection	$9.95
00702228	Neil Young – Greatest Hits	$12.99
00702188	Essential ZZ Top	$10.95

Prices, contents and availability subject to change without notice.

FOR MORE INFORMATION, SEE YOUR LOCAL MUSIC DEALER,
OR WRITE TO:

HAL•LEONARD®
CORPORATION

7777 W. BLUEMOUND RD. P.O. BOX 13819 MILWAUKEE, WI 53213

Visit Hal Leonard online at **www.halleonard.com**

0709